The
Diamond Sutra
or
Prajna-Paramita
(1912)

William Gimmel

ISBN 0-7661-0554-7

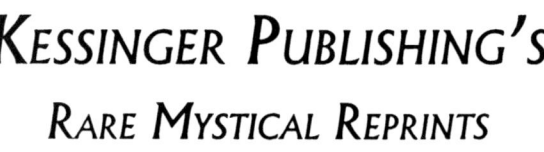

THE
DIAMOND SUTRA
(*CHIN-KANG-CHING*)

OR

PRAJNA-PARAMITA

TRANSLATED FROM THE CHINESE
WITH AN INTRODUCTION AND NOTES

BY

WILLIAM GEMMELL

LONDON
KEGAN PAUL, TRENCH, TRÜBNER & CO., LTD.
BROADWAY HOUSE, 68-74 CARTER LANE, E.C.
1912

THIS VOLUME

IS RESPECTFULLY INSCRIBED TO

MY FRIEND

WILLIAM NIVEN, Esq.,

BY

THE AUTHOR.

PREFACE

This English version of *The Diamond Sutra*,[1] translated from the Chinese text of Kumarajiva, owes its inception to successive conversations with a friend, profoundly interested in the interpretation of oriental systems of philosophy. During those conversations renderings into English were made of numerous passages from the works of Confucius, Mencius, and Lao-Tsz.

Having surveyed briefly those fertile fields of thought, we passed, by a natural transition, into the delectable Buddhist realm. Some passages from the *Chinese Sutras*, comprising texts and annotations, were consecutively examined, and variously considered. Eventually it was suggested that *The Diamond Sutra*, perhaps one of the most metaphysical of the works ascribed to Buddha, be conveniently rendered into the English language.

In order that the rather unfamiliar text might assume due intelligibility, parallel passages and numerous annotations were subjoined, as the pleasant work of translating proceeded. The idea of printing and publishing the text seemed to follow as a natural sequence.

[1] A learned Chinese commentator thus explained the rather striking title: "As the diamond exceeds all other precious gems in brilliance and indestructibility; so, also, does the *wisdom* of *The Diamond Sutra* transcend, and shall outlive, all other knowledge known to philosophy."

PREFACE

Already there exist in the English language, renderings of *The Diamond Sutra* from the Sanscrit by Max Müller, and from the Chinese by Beal. This new version does not seek to enter into rivalry with those erudite works; and a possible apology which might readily be offered for the publication of this modest volume is, that the scholarly productions of Müller and Beal, in their present forms, are perhaps slightly inaccessible to the general English reader.

It would appear that the peculiar charm of the Buddhist philosophy, and the remarkable purity of the Buddhist faith, are becoming more generally appreciated in Europe. Should this imperfect rendering of *The Diamond Sutra*, even in the faintest degree, confirm this just sense of appreciation, or prove a gentle incentive to further enquiry, then its unexpected publication may prove to be not entirely unjustified.

In recording our many obligations to those scholars whose works were frequently consulted, we also give expression to a hope that nothing of importance is omitted which ought to be gratefully acknowledged.

It may also be permissible to express admiration of the piety, and appreciation of the friendship, of those learned monks in Central China, to whom we are everlastingly indebted for even a slight initiation into those inexhaustible truths, which are alike the heritage, and the glory, of the disciples of Buddha. Amongst those we should like to specify are Chang-Ming, the chief monk (Seng-Kwan) of Chen-Chou prefecture, Hu-Nan, and the aged and affectionate Chioh-Hsien.

WM. GEMMELL.

POLLOKSHIELDS, GLASGOW,
6th September 1912.

INTRODUCTION

The Diamond Sutra is one of the most valued and widely read philosophical works in Buddhist literature. It is very popular amongst ardent Buddhists in China, and excepting the *Lotus of the Good Law*, and the *Leng-Yen-Ching*,[1] perhaps no other Sutra ascribed to Buddha is regarded by the Chinese with so great esteem.

In Japan, *The Diamond Sutra* appears to be perused extensively by what Max Müller[2] termed the Shin-Gon sect, founded by Ko-Bo, a disciple of the renowned pilgrim Hiuen-Tsang, about the year 816 A.D.

The Diamond Sutra was written originally in Sanscrit, and in process of time translated into the Tibetan, Chinese, Mongol, and Manchu languages. It represents the Mahayana school of Buddhist thought, a school founded by Nagardjuna,[3] which flourished primarily at

---

[1] "The Sutra of firm establishment in all doctrine, describing clearly the secret merit and attainments in the religious life of Tathagata." (Compare Edkins' *Chinese Buddhism*.)

[2] *See* the preface to *The Vagrakkhedika*.

[3] "A native of Western India who lived as a hermit under an Arguna tree, whence he derived his name. Converted by Kapimala, he laboured in Southern India as the fourteenth patriarch. . . . He is the chief representative, if not originator, of the Mahayana school, the

INTRODUCTION

Tchakuka, and thereafter influenced appreciably a considerable part of the Buddhist Church.

In the year 1836, Csomo Körösi published an account of the Tibetan translation, which interesting document may be consulted in Vol. XX. of the *Asiatic Researches*. *The Diamond Sutra* is therein designated "The Sutra of Wonderful Effects," a treatise by means of which Sakyamuni Buddha instructs Subhuti, one of his conspicuous disciples, in *The Prajna - Paramita* of transcendent wisdom.[1]

To Kumarajiva,[2] a native of Kashmir, who gained

---

greatest philosopher of the Buddhists, and as such styled 'one of the four suns which illuminate the world.' His own peculiar tenets have been perpetuated by a distinct metaphysical school called Madhyamika (*Lit.* Juste Milieu), the characteristics of which are a sophistic nihilism which dissolves every proposition into a thesis and its antithesis, and denies both. 'The soul,' said Nagardjuna, 'has neither existence nor non-existence, it is neither eternal nor non-eternal, neither annihilated by death nor nonannihilated.' The tenets of this school are condensed in Nagardjuna's commentary on the Mahaprajna Paramita S'astra. He spent the later part of his life in a monastery at Kosala . . . (correct date probably A.D. 194). After his death he received the title Bodhisattva. He is the author of many S'atras." (Compare Eitel's *Handbook of Chinese Buddhism*.)

[1] *See* the preface to *The Vagrakkhedika*.

[2] Kumarajiva was referred to as "one of the four suns of Buddhism" (Tchatvara Suryas). He laboured in China as a most active and judicious translator, and is credited with having introduced a new alphabet. One of Kumarajiva's Chinese designations—Tung-Sheo—meant that, although young in years, he was ripe in the wisdom and virtues of old age. (Compare Eitel's *Handbook of Chinese Buddhism*.)

INTRODUCTION

distinction as a monk of the later Chin dynasty[1] (A.D. 384-417), is conceded the honour of having first translated *The Diamond Sutra* into the Chinese language. Of subsequent Chinese translations, perhaps the most noteworthy is the text ascribed to the scholarly *Hiuen-Tsang*, and completed about the middle of the seventh century.[2]

A rendering into English of Kumarajiva's Chinese translation was accomplished by the Rev. S. Beal, and published in *The Journal of the Royal Asiatic Society*, 1864-65. The text and German translation of the Tibetan version were published in 1873 by M. Schmidt, in *The Mémoires de l'Académie St Pétersbourg*. The Mongolian translation was presented by the Baron de Constadt to the library of the Institut de France. The Manchu translation is in the possession of M. de Harlez, who, with the aid of the Tibetan, Manchu, and Chinese versions, published a French translation of the Sanscrit text of *The Diamond Sutra* in the *Journal Asiatique*, 1892.[3] It has been observed[4] that "at first sight it may seem as

---

[1] Beal stated in his preface to the *Kin-Kong-King*, that "it was translated first into the Chinese by Kumara-Jiva (A.D. 405), who was brought into China from Thibet."

[2] Other translations, worthy of recognition, are those attributed respectively to Bodhiruki (A.D. 509), Paramartha (A.D. 562), Dharmagupa, of the Sui dynasty (A.D. 589-618), and I-Tsing (A.D. 703). (Compare the preface to *The Vagrakkhedika*.)

[3] This information may be found in Max Müller's *Vagrakkhedika*, and represented, doubtless, at the period when it was written, a considerable part of the knowledge available on the subject.

[4] By Max Müller.

INTRODUCTION

if this metaphysical treatise hardly deserved the world-wide reputation which it has attained." Regarding this descriptive "world-wide reputation," devout Buddhists might suggest in extenuation, that throughout many centuries, the "spiritual wisdom" of *The Diamond Sutra* produced in countless minds a "conscious blessedness of perfect peace." This "spiritual wisdom" also appeared to be a "strong incentive to holiness," and a grateful inspiration to those who had entered "the path which leads to Nirvana." In a few renowned monasteries of Central China, our Buddhist friends frequently affirmed that, by contemplating the "spiritual wisdom" of *The Diamond Sutra*, the mind would inevitably become "transfused with the mellow light of imperishable truth."

In the preface to *The Vagrakkhedika*, Max Müller made a critical observation regarding certain peculiarities of "'style' adopted in this treatise by the Buddhist philosophers who wished to convince their hearers of the truth of their philosophy." From the Sanscrit text, perhaps it is difficult to realise fully what Asvaghocha[1] described as the "persuasiveness of Buddha's eloquence";[2] yet we may quite appreciate the academic instinct of Kumarajiva, whose work on *The Diamond Sutra* bears evidence of a laudable endeavour to produce a classic, which in the Chinese language is almost entirely beyond reproach.

In all our aspirations to translate or to interpret Buddhist texts, perhaps it might prove advantageous to

[1] The Chinese Ma-Ming.
[2] Compare the Chinese text of the Chi-Sin-Pien—*The Awakening of Faith*.

INTRODUCTION   xiii

bear in mind the significant words incorporated in the *Light of Asia*:—

"*And time hath blurred their script and ancient sense,
Which once was new and mighty, moving all.*"

Max Müller stated [1] that *The Diamond Sutra* represents at reatise on "metaphysical agnosticism," and he excused its "endless repetition of the same process of reasoning" on the assumption, that the subject-matter of the *Sutra* was probably "perfectly familiar to children and ignorant persons."

By referring to our Chinese text, we are led to suppose that *The Diamond Sutra* was "delivered expressly for those who had entered the Path which leads to Nirvana," and for those who are "attaining to the ultimate plane of Buddhic thought." Our Chinese annotators also appear to be unanimous in suggesting, that the "spiritual wisdom" of *The Diamond Sutra* is understood only in its rudimentary forms, by those of immature or uninitiated mind.

Concerning what has been termed the "agnosticism" of *The Diamond Sutra*, Sakyamuni Buddha, when he admissibly delivered the text, indicated clearly that there is a sense in which the "highest perfect knowledge" [2] may be referred to as "unknown." Dante appears to have had a similar difficulty regarding "knowledge" and "power" wherewith to express the higher forms of spiritual experience; and the following lines, constituting the opening stanzas of *The Paradiso*, may serve to elucidate the Buddhist position,

[1] In the preface to *The Vagrakkhedika*.
[2] "Supreme spiritual wisdom." In Beal's *Kin-Kong-King*, "The unsurpassed, just, and enlightened heart." (Sanscrit, "*Annuttara Samyak Sambodhi Hridaya.*")

INTRODUCTION

and make it perhaps more intelligible to those who are as yet unfamiliar with its peculiar modes of thought:—

> "*La gloria di colui che tutto move*
> *Per l'universo penetra, e risplende*
> *In una parte più, e meno altrove.*
>
> "*Nel ciel che più della sua luce prende*
> *Fu'io; e vidi cose che ridire*
> *Nè sa nè può qual di lassù discende;*
>
> "*Perchè, appressando sè al suo disire,*
> *Nostro intelletto*[1] *si profonda tanto,*
> *Che retro la memoria non può ire.*"[2]

In order to appreciate fully the philosophy of *The Diamond Sutra*, doubtless it is necessary to interpret aright the meaning of the Buddhist terminology. In this connection, the Sanscrit Dharma—usually rendered into Chinese by "Fah," and into English by "Law"—appears to merit our immediate attention.

Max Müller, with his ample knowledge, stated that Dharma, "in the ordinary Buddhist phraseology, may be correctly rendered by Law; and thus the whole teaching of Buddha is named *Saddharma* — 'The Good Law.' What *The Diamond Sutra* wishes to teach is that all objects, differing one from the other by their Dharmas, are illusive,

---

[1] According to the text of *The Diamond Sutra*, the intellect of Sakyamuni Buddha sank so profoundly into the past, that he was enabled to speak confidently of his experiences in previous incarnations. (Compare pp. 56, 57.)

[2] From the text adopted by Mr H. Oelsner, M.A., Ph.D., for *The Temple Classics*.

INTRODUCTION

or as we should say, phenomenal and subjective, that they are, in fact, of our own making, the products of our own mind." With those noteworthy observations, there is embodied in the preface to *The Vagrakkhedika*, the following interesting suggestion, that the Greek εἶδος—whatever is seen, form, shape, figure—appears to be the equivalent of the Sanscrit Dharma.

Spence Hardy, a distinguished writer on Buddhism, made a suggestion of perhaps equal importance, with reference to the correct interpretation of Dharma. In his well-known volume *Eastern Monachism*, there occurs the following relevant passage: "The second of the three great treasures is called Dhammo, or in Singhalese Dharmma. This word has various meanings, but is here to be understood in the sense of *truth*."

Rhys Davids in his useful volume *Buddhism*, indicated that "Dharma (Pali Dhamma) is not law, but that which underlies and includes the law — a word often most difficult to translate, but best rendered here by Truth and Righteousness."[1]

Perhaps it may be opportune to remark, that had Kumarajiva regarded "form," "truth," or "righteousness,"

---

[1] Dr Edkins, in his scholarly work *Chinese Buddhism*, seems to have regarded "the Law or body of doctrine" as an accurate definition of Dharma.

Dr Eitel, in his *Handbook of Chinese Buddhism*, explained Dharma by "Fah" — "Law"; and observed that it is "a general term for religious objects, especially for the Buddhistic Canon."

Mr Vincent A. Smith, in *Asoka, Buddhist Emperor of India*, suggested that the Chinese *Hsiao* (piety), and the Latin Pietas, coincide with the Sanscrit term Dharma.

as expressing adequately the Sancrit Dharma, these familiar terms being obviously at his command, might have been utilised at pleasure. Like the cultured Asvaghocha, Kumarajiva may have regarded the "nature" of the Law as "co-extensive with the illimitable ocean of being";[1] and within that ample compass, perhaps he thought there might synthetically be included those beautifully-defined concepts "form," "truth," and "righteousness."

Chinese annotators of *The Diamond Sutra* seldom criticise adversely its classic terminology, or suggest many inapplicable alternative renderings. They appear to have surveyed the realm of "spiritual wisdom" enunciated by Sakyamuni Buddha, and thereafter to have become greatly impressed by the thought that, in its *Essence*, it might possibly be inexhaustible. This may in part explain their motive for incorporating in the commentary a familiar passage from *Lao-Tsz*, "Infinite truth is inexpressible"[2]—which in a measure illustrates the appreciable difficulty of stating, in exact terms of philosophy, the equivalent of the Buddhic "Law."

In our intercourse with Buddhist monks, we heard the rather engaging suggestion, that the familiar Christian phrase, "the law of the spirit of life," contains a spiritual concept which appears to approximate closely to the idea of the "Law" of Buddha. Those monks seemed to believe that the "Law"[3] enters quietly and operates

---

[1] The Chinese phrase is "Fah-sing-chen-ru-hai."
[2] *See* the *Tao-Teh-Ching*. Compare, also, the statement attributed to Confucius—"Nature and Truth cannot be adequately expressed."
[3] Or Dharma.

INTRODUCTION xvii

imperceptibly within every natural and spiritual sphere; and that they have at least a semblance of reason for their belief, the following exquisite lines clearly indicate:—

> *"This is its touch upon the blossomed rose,*
> *The fashion of its hand shaped lotus-leaves.*
>
> *"That is its painting on the glorious clouds,*
> *And these its emeralds on the peacock's train.*
>
> *"Out of the dark it wrought the heart of man,*
> *Out of dull shells the pheasant's pencilled neck.*
>
> *"It spreadeth forth for flight the eagle's wings*
> *What time she beareth home her prey.*
>
> *"This is its work upon the things ye see*
> *The unseen things are more; men's hearts and minds,*
> *The thoughts of peoples and their ways and wills,*
> *Those, too, the great Law binds."* [1]

As we consider the manifold operations of this "Law which moves to righteousness," perhaps we may gradually appreciate the dignified mind of Sakyamuni, when he addressed Subhuti, saying: "What is usually referred to as the 'Law' of Buddha, is not in reality a 'Law' attributive to Buddha, it is merely termed the 'Law' of Buddha." [2]

---

[1] Compare *The Light of Asia*. Perhaps this aspect of the "Law" of Buddha may be conceived of as harmonising with Shakespeare's idea of a "Divinity."

[2] It may be interesting to observe that, according to our Chinese text, Sakyamuni Buddha evidently disclaimed any desire to formulate, or to perpetuate, a stereotyped system of "Law" or "doctrine." Sakyamuni Buddha also made it plain, that the "Law" which he enunciated, was presented

xviii   INTRODUCTION

The Sanscrit term Samgna,[1] usually rendered into Chinese by "Ming," and into English by "Name," seems to deserve our further attention. Like the term Dharma, a clear knowledge of "Samgna" is indispensable for a correct understanding of our text.

In one of the opening passages of *The Diamond Sutra*, we find that Sakyamuni Buddha, in reply to an enquiry by Subhuti, suggests that by means of this "wisdom," enlightened disciples shall be enabled to bring into subjection every inordinate desire.

"*Every species of life, whether hatched in the egg, formed in the womb, evolved from spawn, produced by metamorphosis, with or without form or intelligence, possessing or devoid of natural instinct—from these changeful conditions of being*

before the minds of his disciples in the simile of a "raft"— a thing to be abandoned when the mind "touched the further shore" of everlasting truth. It seems to be in this tentative sense that intellectual Buddhists regard all ecclesiastical institutions, priesthoods, dogmas, ordinances, etc.; and we have met monks who would classify "belief in the "efficacy" of religious rites or ceremonies, with obnoxious forms of "heresy" and "immorality." (Compare Rhys Davids' *Buddhism*.) With regard to the Buddhist objection concerning the "efficacy" of religious "rites," compare the noble sentiments expressed in the following lines, delightfully rendered by Sir Edwin Arnold from the *Bhagavad-Gita* (*The Song Celestial*):—

"Serenity of soul, benignity,
 Sway of the silent spirit, constant stress
 To sanctify the nature,—these things make
 Good rite, and true religiousness of mind."

[1] Max Müller suggests that Samgna and Dharma "correspond in many respects to the Vedantic Namarupe" —in Chinese Ming-Seh—name, form, or characteristic.

INTRODUCTION

I command you to seek deliverance in the transcendental concept of Nirvana. Thus you shall obtain deliverance from the idea of an immeasurable, innumerable, and illimitable world of sentient life; but, in reality there is no idea of a world of sentient life from which to obtain deliverance. And why? Because, in the mind of an enlightened disciple, there have ceased to exist such arbitrary ideas of phenomena as an entity, a being, a living being, or a personality."

A similar process of reasoning appears to permeate the whole of *The Diamond Sutra*, and whether appertaining to a living being,[1] a virtue,[2] a condition of mind,[3] a Buddhist kingdom,[4] or a personal Buddha,[5] there is implied in each concept a spiritual essence, only imperfectly described, if not entirely overlooked, in the ordinary use of each particular name. Shakespeare enquired, "What's in a name?" and in a thought inspired by the rose and its delicious fragrance, suggested with Buddha, that there is little, or nothing, in a name which explains the real nature of an object. Even a "particle of dust" seems, to the Buddhist mind, to embody in its composition a subtle spiritual element, entirely "inscrutable," and quite "incomprehensible."

According to the Mahayana School of Buddhist thought, objects and their respective names are alike unreal and illusory. Objects and names, in the abstract, represent merely the products of untutored and unenlightened minds. Nothing is real, in the sense that it is permanent. Everything appears to be subject to irrevocable Laws of change and decay. As the things which we see are temporal, it

[1] Compare p. 86. [2] Compare p. 55. [3] Compare p. 80.
[4] Compare p. 76. [5] Compare p. 95.

is essential for our intellectual development, that we focus our thoughts upon the things which are Unseen and Eternal. Many minds are susceptible of deception by the fleeting phenomena of life; but behind these phenomena there is an essential element, entirely spiritual,[1] uninfluenced by arbitrary ideas or changeful conditions, which "pervades all things," and is "pure" and "unchanging."

Perhaps it might prove of interest to quote the following outline of Mahayana doctrine[2] prepared by Mr S. Kuroda, which was approved by several influential Buddhist communions in Japan, "and published with authority at Tokyo in 1893":—

"All things that are produced by causes and conditions are inevitably destined to extinction. There is nothing that has any reality; when conditions come things begin to appear, when conditions cease these things likewise cease to exist. Like the foam of the water, like the lightning flash,[3] and like the floating, swiftly vanishing clouds, they are only of momentary duration. As all things have no constant nature of their own, so there is no actuality in pure and impure, rough and fine, large and small, far and near, knowable and unknowable, etc On this account it is sometimes said that all things are nothing. The apparent phenomena around us are, however, produced by mental operations within us, and thus distinctions are established. . . .

"All things are included under subject and object. The

---

[1] Some modern Japanese Buddhists appear to regard this purely spiritual element as "essence of mind."
[2] From the preface to *The Vagrakkhedika*.
[3] Compare p. 110.

subject is an entity in which mental operations are awakened whenever there are objects, while the object consists of all things, visible and invisible, knowable and unknowable, etc. The subject is not something that occupies some space in the body alone, nor does the object exist outside of the subject. . . .[1]

"The various phenomena which appear as subjects and objects are divided into two kinds:—the perceptible and knowable, the imperceptible and unknowable. . . . Now, what are the imperceptible and unknowable phenomena?

"Through the influence of habitual delusions, boundless worlds, innumerable varieties of things spring up in the mind. This boundless universe and these subtle ideas are not perceptible and knowable;[2] only Bodhisattvas[3] believe, understand, and become perfectly convinced of these through the contemplation of Vidyamatara[4] (all things are nothing but phenomena in mind); hence they are called imperceptible and unknowable. What are the perceptible and knowable phenomena?

"Not knowing that these imperceptible and unknowable phenomena are the productions of their own minds, men from their habitual delusions invest them with an existence

[1] Compare the interesting dialogue entitled *The Enlightenment of Ananda*, in which Sakyamuni instructs his distinguished disciple in ideas concerning the subjective and objective phenomena of mind.

[2] Compare pp. 102, 103.

[3] Bodhisattvas—greatly enlightened disciples.

[4] *Vidya Matra Siddhi*, a philosophical work by Vasubandhu, a native of Radjagriha, and disciple of Nagarjuna, founder of the Mahayana school. (Compare Eitel's *Handbook of Chinese Buddhism*.)

outside of mind, as perceptible mental phenomena, as things visible, audible, etc. These phenomena are called perceptible and knowable.

"Though there are thus two kinds, perceptible and imperceptible phenomena, they occur upon the same things, and are inseparably bound together even in the smallest particle. Their difference in appearance is caused only by differences, both in mental phenomena and in the depth of conviction. Those who know only the perceptible things, without knowing the imperceptible, are called the unenlightened by Buddha. . . .

"In contradistinction to the fallacious phenomena, there is the true Essence of Mind. Underlying the phenomena of mind, there is an unchanging principle which we call essence of mind. . . . The essence of mind is the entity without ideas and without phenomena, and is always the same. It pervades all things, and is pure and unchanging. . . . The essence and the phenomena of mind are inseparable; and as the former is all-pervading and ever-existing, so the phenomena occur everywhere and continually, wherever suitable conditions accompany it. Thus the perceptible and imperceptible phenomena are manifestations of the essence of mind that, according to the number and nature of conditions, develop without restraint. All things in the universe, therefore, are mind itself.

"By this we do not mean that all things combine into a mental unity called mind, nor that all things are emanations from it, but that, without changing their places or appearance, they are mind itself everywhere. Buddha saw this truth and said that the whole universe was his own. Hence it is clear that where the essence of mind is found, and the necessary conditions accompany it, the phenomena of mind never fail to appear. . . . Though there is a distinction between the essence and the phenomena of mind, yet they are nothing but one and the same substance, that is, *mind*. So we say that there exists nothing but mind. Though both the world of the pure and impure, and the generation of all things, are very wide and deep, yet they owe their existence to our mind."

Perhaps we might appropriately indicate that however interesting, or even fascinating, may be the nice distinction between *mind* and *essence of mind*, in relation to phenomena, so far as we are aware, the distinction may be implied, but is never precisely stated, in the text of *The Diamond Sutra*. Nevertheless, we may readily appreciate the subtle intellectual movement, which endeavours to distinguish clearly between the phenomena of mind, and an unchanging principle underlying it, capable of being defined as Essence of Mind. Yet we have a notion that our Japanese Buddhist friends intuitively find in their beautiful concept, infinitely more of a purely spiritual nature, than they attempt to express by the mere metaphysical term. Doubtless they have frequently applied to it the incisive logic of Sakyamuni Buddha, and found simultaneously, that what is ordinarily referred to as "essence of mind," is not in reality "essence of mind," it is merely termed "essence of mind."[1]

[1] Compare the process of reasoning which permeates the entire *Diamond Sutra*. We hope no injustice is done to our Japanese friends, by applying to their beautiful concept "essence of mind," this familiar logical method of Sakyamuni Buddha.

The term Buddha, as defined in *The Diamond Sutra*, seems to merit a brief consideration. In fulfilment of our present purpose, it seems almost unnecessary to enter into questions regarding the historical Buddha, or to the authenticity of Sutras ascribed to his genius. Therefore, without indicating any particular reservation, we meantime accept the traditional statements that the Buddha of *The Diamond Sutra* was the son of Suddhodana, the husband of Yasodhara, and the father of Rahula. But, incorporated with the text, there is embodied in the familiar term Buddha, a lofty spiritual concept, which seems to place it in a category where fresh interest is imparted to the question of its interpretation.

Concluding the twenty-sixth chapter of *The Diamond Sutra*, wherein "the spiritual[1] body is entirely differentiated from external phenomena," Sakyamuni, in reply to an enquiry regarding the possibility of perceiving "Buddha" by means of his bodily distinctions, delivered the following remarkable Gatha[2]:—

I am not to be perceived by means of any visible form,
Nor sought after by means of any audible sound;
Whosoever walks in the way of iniquity,
Cannot perceive the blessedness of the Lord Buddha.[3]

---

[1] Fah-Shen—the Law, or spiritual body. Compare Shen-Shen, the term usually employed in the Chinese rendering of the New Testament Scriptures to denote the spiritual body.

[2] Gatha—usually a Scripture verse comprising four lines.

[3] Compare the following lines from *The Song Celestial*:—
"I am not known
To evil-doers, . . . nor to those
Whose mind is cheated by the show of things."

INTRODUCTION

In the twenty-ninth chapter of *The Diamond Sutra*, wherein is expounded "the majesty of the absolute," Sakyamuni declared that a disciple who affirms that "Buddha" comes or goes, obviously has not understood the meaning of his instruction. Because, as we learn from our text, the idea "Buddha" implies neither coming from anywhere, nor going to anywhere. This purely spiritual concept of Buddha seems to have seized the imagination, and inspired the writer of the *Yuen-Chioh Sutra*,[1] to whom are ascribed the following significant lines:—

"*Like drifting clouds, like the waning moon, like ships that sail the ocean, like shores that are washed away—these are symbolic of endless change. But the blessed Buddha, in his essential, absolute nature, is changeless and everlasting.*"

Again, in the seventeenth chapter of *The Diamond Sutra*, it is declared that in the word "Buddha," every Law is intelligibly comprehended.[2] To Western minds, it might become necessary to resist a natural inclination to ascribe to those elements of thought, an influence which had its

---

[1] In Buddhist phraseology, Yuen - Chioh means the study, by means of contemplation, of primary spiritual causes.

[2] Compare Beal's rendering in the *Kin - Kong - King*, "Tathagata is the explanation as it were of all systems of Law." *See* also *The Book of the Manifesting of the One and Manifold* in *The Song Celestial*, the verse commencing:—

"Thou, of all souls the Soul!
The comprehending whole!"

In conversation with Chinese monks regarding the meaning of this impressive passage, we found that they invariably approved of a suggested rendering, that "Buddha is the *One* in whom all Laws become intelligible."

inception in a nation other than the Indian.[1] But, lest we should appear to detract from the native glory of Sakyamuni Buddha, perhaps it might prove opportune to remark, that there is sufficient evidence in the ancient Vedic hymns, Upanishads, etc., to indicate clearly the probable starting-points in the evolution of his thought. It seems to be to the everlasting honour of some early Indian philosophers, that they endeavoured carefully to combine in an abstract spiritual unity, all the essential elements usually comprehended under the term "Divinity."[2] This may in a manner explain why the devout Buddhist, possessing a natural mental tendency — induced by persistent Hindoo influence—is enabled to regard "Buddha"[3] in a purely spiritual sense, as the One[4] in whom all Laws are comprehended and become perfectly intelligible.

In *The Diamond Sutra* it may be observed that incidental

[1] Compare the observations made by Sir Edwin Arnold in his preface to *The Song Celestial*, regarding the date when that famous Brahmanic poem was composed; and the gentle indication that in its teaching may be found "echoes of the lessons of Galilee, and of the Syrian incarnation."

[2] An instructive exposition of this subject by J. Muir, Esq., entitled *The Progress of the Vedic Religion towards Abstract Conceptions of the Deity*, may be consulted in the *Jour. R.A.S.*, 1864-65.

[3] In colloquial Chinese there is a noteworthy saying, that "Buddha is simply a condition of mind." This "condition of mind" is beautifully expressed by a "classic" couplet, which, rendered into English, means "as pure as the image of the moon in a river," and "as lovely as the bloom of a flower in a mirror" (Shui-Li-Chï-Yüeh, Ching-Li-Chï-Wha).

[4] Compare the beautifully-expressed sentiment of Akhnaton, Pharaoh of Egypt, concerning "the One in whom all Laws are intelligibly comprehended." "There is no poverty for him who hath Thee in his heart." (See *Life and Times of Akhnaton*.)

reference is made by Sakyamuni Buddha to the doctrines of Karma and Reincarnation. It seems to be an old truth to which expression is given in the *Epistle to the Galatians*: "Whatsoever a man soweth, that shall he also reap. For he that soweth to his flesh shall of the flesh reap corruption; but he that soweth to the Spirit shall of the Spirit reap life everlasting."[1]

To the Buddhist mind, Karma is indissolubly associated with "the Law which moves to Righteousness." Thus it is accustomed to view the traditional Christian idea of "justification by Faith," rather as a devoutly-conceived theory, than as a reasonably-constructed truth.

Occasionally we have heard a gentle affirmation, that the Western mind seems unwittingly inclined to confound the doctrine of Karma with a concept which is almost suggestive of Fatalism. If Karma contains even a germ of thought which corresponds to "blind fatalism," the idea is perhaps quite felicitously expressed in the following sentences, culled from a valued letter written by an aged Chinese monk: "Karma is a universal Law which gently binds us to the rhythmic cycle of evolving life. It

[1] Rhys Davids, when he expounded the doctrine of Karma in *Buddhism*, clearly indicated the Buddhist position, "that whatever a man reaps, that he must also have sown." Chinese Buddhists appear to be assured, ' 'that if a man reaps sorrow, disappointment, pain, he himself, and no other, must at some time have sown folly, error, sin; and if not in this life, then in some former birth. Where then, in the latter case, is the identity between him who sows and him who reaps? *In that which alone remains* when a man dies, and the constituent parts of the sentient being are dissolved; in the result, namely, of his action, speech, and thought, in his good or evil *Karma* (literally his 'doing') which *does not* die."

operates so quietly and imperceptibly that we scarcely are conscious of its presence. The absolute truth of Karma greatly attracts our minds, which approve naturally of its consummate justice and perfect righteousness."

Those ideas of "consummate justice" and "perfect righteousness," seem to be faithfully portrayed in the following quotation, gleaned from *The Light of Asia* :—

"*What hath been bringeth what shall be, and is,*
Worse—better—last for first and first for last :
The Angels in the Heavens of Gladness reap
Fruits of a holy past."

It would therefore appear that Karma may be regarded generally, as comprising the constituent moral elements derived consecutively from the thoughts, words, and actions of an interminable life's cycle. Perhaps it is in this connection that Chinese Buddhists frequently assume Karma to resemble "a moral fibre, indissolubly entwined in sentient life." It may be believed to recede far into the past, and to extend indefinitely into the future.

Although realising the significance of Karma,[1] the devout Buddhist mind is not usually disturbed by fearful forebodings. Ostensibly, it has evolved to a condition of holiness, wherein "the dross of sin" is entirely consumed in the "white flames" of Sakyamuni's "transcendent wisdom" and "boundless love."

Within the realm of Buddhist philosophy, the doctrine of re-incarnation is conspicuous by reason of its peculiarly

[1] In the concept Karma, Sakyamuni Buddha suggested the revealing of a *moral cause* which explained the otherwise insoluble riddle of the evident inequalities, and consequent sufferings of life.

attractive charms. On first acquaintance, the European mind may be somewhat "startled" to discover, that a satisfactory explanation of the interminable evolution of life, is sought for by the earnest Buddhist in the theory of reincarnation.

In the text of *The Diamond Sutra*, it may be observed that Sakyamuni Buddha, in discoursing to Subhuti, referred incidentally to personal reminiscences, one of which belonged to a distant period of five hundred incarnations.

According to the text of *The Light of Asia*, the spiritual consciousness of Sakyamuni Buddha extended to a period even more remote, as may be judged by these remarkable lines :—

> "*I now remember*, *myriad* rains *ago*,
> *What time I roamed Himâla's hanging woods.*"

In considering briefly the doctrine of reincarnation, perhaps it might readily be conceded to our Buddhist friends, that there were exemplified in the Founder of their faith, a wonderful potency of intellect, and a marvellous degree of spiritual intuition. Quite agreeable, also, may be the suggestion, that this potency of intellect might become intensified, and probably "rendered subjective," by "ascetic exercises," abstract contemplation, and "determined effort."

Spence Hardy indicated in *Eastern Monachism* that the Buddhist mind conceives of "spiritual powers" arising from the aforementioned "potency of intellect" and "spiritual intuition," which in other systems of religion are usually regarded as partaking of the nature of "Divinity." If it be admitted that those potential "powers" are probably susceptible of affiliation with the Divine Spirit, then the way of approach to an understanding of the Buddhist theory of intuition becomes, perhaps, tolerably clear. Concrete knowledge acquired by intuition, appears to assure our Buddhist friends of the *fact* of reincarnation. But they invariably refrain from a vain attempt to *prove* the "fact," by an authorised—and consequently stereotyped—process of reasoning.

The unknown Hindoo author of *The Bhagavad-Gita* revealed in simple phraseology the native idea of reincarnation; and suggested, happily, an instructive theory concerning the advent of great Teachers and Saviours in every age. To Krishna are ascribed the following sayings;—

"*Manifold the renewals of my birth*
Have been. . . . When Righteousness
Declines, O Bharata, when Wickedness
Is strong, I rise, from age to age, and take
Visible shape, and move a man with men,
Succouring the good, thrusting the evil back,
And setting Virtue on her seat again."

Rhys Davids justly observed that "to the pious Buddhist it is a constant source of joy and gratitude that 'the Buddha,' not only then, but in many former births, when emancipation from all the cares and troubles of life was already within his reach, should again and again, in mere love for man, have condescended to enter the world, and live amidst the sorrows inseparable from finite existence."[1] Perhaps in a more general sense the idea of reincarnation appealed strongly to the imagination of

[1] Compare *Buddhism*.

Wordsworth, when he was inspired to write these familiar, yet exquisite, lines :—

> *"Our birth is but a sleep and a forgetting;*
> *The soul that rises with us, our life's star,*
> *Hath had elsewhere its setting*
> *And cometh from afar."*

Regarding the doctrines of Individuality and non-Individuality, which characterise the text of *The Diamond Sutra*, wherein are found to occur frequently Chinese equivalents for the ordinary concepts of an entity, a being, a living being and a personality, the following passage from *The Bhagavad-Gita*, suggestive almost of complete harmony with the Buddhist doctrine, may serve to make even a cursory consideration of the subject perhaps more illuminating. The passage, rendered by Sir Edwin Arnold, is as follows :—

> *"There is 'true' Knowledge, Learn it thou in this:*
> *To see one changeless Life in all the Lives,*
> *And in the Separate, One Inseparable.*
> *There is imperfect Knowledge: that which sees*
> *The separate existences apart,*
> *And, being separated, holds them real."*

As Nirvana is only referred to casually in *The Diamond Sutra*, that familiar Buddhist term hardly calls for any present detailed explanation. Within a brief compass probably no better explanation may be forthcoming than what is already given in this concise exposition gathered from *The Light of Asia* :—

> *"If any teach Nirvana is to cease,*
> *Say unto such they lie."*

xxxii   INTRODUCTION

"*If any teach Nirvana is to live,
Say unto such they err; not knowing this,
Nor what light shines beyond their broken lamps,
Nor lifeless, timeless bliss.*"

In concluding, it might be opportune to observe, that the *Werthurtheile*,[1] known amongst modern theologians as characterising the teaching of Albrecht Ritschl—sounds, upon intimate acquaintance, merely as a faint echo of the logic of Sakyamuni Buddha. Ritschl might apply his *Werthurtheile* to the presumed interpretation of a "miracle," etc. Buddha suggested by his "method," that what is ordinarily referred to as a "miracle," is not in *reality* a "miracle," therefore it is merely *defined* as a "miracle." So, also, with the various dogmas which distinguish every religious creed. By many Chinese it is regarded as an evidence of Divinity, that in the mind of Sakyamuni Buddha there was conceived this incisive logical method; and amongst the learned monks, profound homage is rendered, and much wonder expressed, because the Lord Buddha[2] did not hesitate to apply its principles to every doctrine synonymous with his own accredited "Law."

[1] "The much-canvassed Ritschlian doctrine of the *Worth*—or 'value-judgments,' in which the peculiarity of religious knowledge is supposed to lie." For the introduction of the term into theology we are indebted to Herrmann, *Die Religion*, etc., and Kaftan, *Das Wesen*. *See* Orr's, *The Ritschlian Theology and The Evangelical Faith*.

[2] It may be observed in this English version of *The Diamond Sutra*, that the Chinese term *Fuh*, in deference to our Oriental friends, is invariably rendered "Lord Buddha"—a designation consonant with *their* concepts of devotion and piety.

THE DIAMOND SUTRA

THUS have I heard[1] concerning our Lord Buddha:—

Upon a memorable occasion, the Lord Buddha[2] sojourned in the kingdom of

---

[1] It is generally supposed that the familiar introductory phrase, "Thus have I heard," was adopted by the writers or editors of Buddhist Sutras in order that their scriptures might assume the same high degree of authority as the Brahmanas and the Mantras, "as forming the 'S'ruti' or sacred revelation of the followers of the Vedas." (Compare Max Müller's *History of Sanscrit Literature* and the valuable note in Beal's *Kin-Kong-King*.)

[2] "The term (Buddha) means 'every intelligent being who has thrown off the bondage of sense perception and self, knows the utter unreality of all phenomena, and is ready to enter Nirvana.'"—*Handbook of Chinese Buddhism*. EITEL.

Shravasti,[1] lodging in the grove of Jeta,[2] a park within the imperial domain, which Jeta, the heir-apparent, bestowed upon Sutana,[3] a

---

[1] Shravasti is variously described as the city (or kingdom) of philosophy, of good doctrine, of abundant virtue, and as the abode of immortals. It was situated on the north bank of the Ganges, about 200 miles above Benares. Much interesting information regarding the sacred city Shravasti, is fortunately preserved in the instructive records of the distinguished Chinese pilgrims, *Fa-Hien* and *Hiuen-Tsang*.

[2] "Prasenajit, the king of Shravasti, was very favourable to the Buddhist religion. It was his minister who bought the garden of Jeta from the prince of that name, and erected in it a residence for Buddha (*see* Julien's *Memoirs sur les Contrées Occidentales*). Many of the Sutras attributed to Buddha are said to have been delivered here. *Hiuen-Tsang* observed the remains of the monastery formerly standing on the site of the garden of Jeta, 2 miles below the city." — *Chinese Buddhism.* EDKINS.

[3] "A person of extraordinary piety and goodness. One of the former Djatakas of Sakyamuni when he was a prince, and forfeited the throne by liberality in almsgiving." —*Handbook of Chinese Buddhism.* EITEL.

benevolent Minister of State, renowned for his charities and benefactions.

With the Lord Buddha, there were assembled together twelve hundred and fifty mendicant disciples,[1] all of whom had attained to eminent degrees of spiritual wisdom.

As it approached the hour for the morning meal, Lord Buddha, Honoured of the Worlds,[2] attired himself in a mendicant's robe,[3] and bearing an alms-bowl in his hands, walked

[1] The Chinese text is *ta-pi-k'u* — greater disciples. Our Chinese editor of *The Diamond Sutra* suggests that there are different grades of discipleship. The "lesser disciples" are those who have abandoned every form of vice, and are striving after virtue. The "greater disciples" are those to whom virtue has become spontaneous, and who have ceased to strive after its attainment.

[2] A title conferred by Chinese Buddhists upon the founder of their faith, believing him to be a Teacher and Saviour whose merit is acclaimed in worlds beyond our own.

[3] Having taken vows of poverty, a robe is one of the following eight articles which Buddhist monks are permitted to possess: three garments of different descriptions, a girdle for the loins, an alms-bowl, a razor, a needle, and a water-strainer.

towards the great city of Shravasti, which he entered to beg for food.[1] Within the city he proceeded from door to door,[2] and received such donations as the good people severally bestowed.[3] Concluding this religious exercise, the Lord Buddha returned to the grove of Jeta, and partook of the frugal meal[4] received

[1] Buddha has said, "the wise priest never asks for anything; he disdains to beg; it is a proper thing for which he carries the alms-bowl; and this is his only mode of solicitation. But when he is sick, he is permitted to ask for any medicine that he may require, without being guilty of any transgression."—*Eastern Monachism.* SPENCE HARDY.

[2] Concerning the manner of begging an alms: "As a bee, injuring not the flower, or its colour, or its scent, flies away, taking the nectar, so let a sage go through the village." —*Questions of King Milinda.* T. W. RHYS DAVIDS.

[3] "By many of the Buddhists it is considered to be an act of great merit to make a vow never to partake of food without giving a portion to the priests."—*Eastern Monachism.* SPENCE HARDY.

[4] "The fifth of the twelve sacred observances of the Chinese is called in Sanscrit Khaloupas' Waddhaktinka, and is said to enjoin that the food obtained by the mendicant is to be divided

as alms. Thereafter he divested himself of his mendicant's robe, laid aside the venerated alms-bowl,[1] bathed his sacred feet, and

into three portions: one to be given to any person whom he sees to be suffering from hunger, and a second to be carried to some quiet place in the forest, and placed upon a stone for the birds and beasts. If he does not meet with any one who is in want, he is not to eat the whole of the food that he has received, but two-thirds only. By this means his body will be lighter and more active. . . . He will be able readily to enter upon the practice of all good works. When any one eats too greedily . . . nothing is more harmful to the development of reason." (Quotation from Remusat's *Relation des Royaumes Buddhiques*, in Spence Hardy's *Eastern Monachism*.)

[1] "The alms-bowl which Sakyamuni used is considered a sacred relic, and to be used by each of the hundred Buddhas of the present kalpa. It was first preserved in Vais'ali, whence its emigrations began to Gandhara, to Persia, to China, to Ceylon, to Madhyades'a, up into the heaven Tuchita, and down to the bottom of the ocean, where it is to await (in the palace of Sagara) the advent of Meitreya Buddha." — *Handbook of Chinese Buddhism*. EITEL.

accepted the honoured seat reserved for him by his disciples.

Upon that occasion, the venerable Subhuti[1] occupied a place in the midst of the assembly. Rising from his seat, with cloak arranged in such manner that his right shoulder was disclosed, Subhuti knelt upon his right knee, then pressing together the palms of his hands, he respectfully raised them towards Lord Buddha, saying: "Thou art of transcendent wisdom, Honoured of the Worlds! With wonderful solicitude, Thou dost preserve in the faith, and instruct in the Law, this illustrious assembly of enlightened disciples.[2]

[1] "A famous dialectician noted for the subtilty of his intellect. He was a native of Shravasti, a contemporary of Sakyamuni, and figures as the principal interlocutor in the *Prajna-Paramita.*"—*Handbook of Chinese Buddhism.* EITEL.

[2] "*Pu-Sa* or Bodhisattva, literally he whose essence (Sattva) has become intelligence (Bodhi). A being that has only once more to pass through human existence before it attains to Buddhaship. The third class of Buddhistic saints comprehending all who are candidates for Buddhaship as well as those

Honoured of the Worlds! if a good disciple, whether man or woman,[1] seeks to obtain supreme spiritual wisdom,[2] what immutable Law shall sustain the mind of that disciple,

Buddhas who are not yet perfected by entrance into Nirvana. They are also styled Mahasattvas (*Mo-Ho-Sa*). The state of a Bodhisattva is considered as one of the three means of conveyance to Nirvana."—*Handbook of Chinese Buddhism.* EITEL.

[1] "Women began to ask and received permission to take the vows. They were called in India Bikshuni. . . . Ni is the Sanscrit feminine termination of Bikshu. These female mendicants were subject to the same code of regulations as the males."—*Chinese Buddhism.* EDKINS.

[2] "*ho-ru-to-lo-san-mao-san-pu-ti* (Anuttara Samyak Sambodhi), literally unexcelled perfect intelligence. Another more painstaking but arbitrary explanation is untarnished and unparalleled (Nuttara) correct view (Sam) and complete wisdom (Myak) with complete possession of the highest sentiments (Sambodhi). This term, one of the sacred phrases of most frequent occurrence, signifies the characteristics which every Buddha possesses."
—*Handbook of Chinese Buddhism.* EITEL.

"The unsurpassed, just, and enlightened heart."—*Kin-Kong-King.* BEAL.

and bring into subjection every inordinate desire?"[1]

The Lord Buddha replied to Subhuti, saying: "Truly a most excellent theme! As you affirmed, I preserve in the faith, and instruct in the Law, this illustrious assembly of enlightened disciples. Attend diligently unto me, and I shall enunciate a Law whereby the mind of a good disciple, whether man or woman, seeking to obtain supreme spiritual wisdom,[2] shall be adequately sustained, and enabled to bring into subjection[3] every inordinate desire." Subhuti was gratified, and signified glad consent. Thereupon, the Lord

---

[1] "When a man's heart is disposed in accordance with his roaming senses, it snatches away his spiritual knowledge as the wind does a ship on the waves."—*Bhagavad-Gita.* J. COCKBURN THOMSON.

[2] Chinese commentators are careful to explain that the title of this Sutra, *Po-ro-po-lo-mi* (*Prajna-Paramita*), means Wisdom, by which we are enabled to reach the other shore (Nirvana).

[3] "Bringing into captivity every thought to the obedience of Christ."—The APOSTLE PAUL.

Buddha, with majesty of person,[1] and perfect articulation, proceeded to deliver the text of this Scripture,[2] saying:—

* * * * *

"By this wisdom shall enlightened disciples be enabled to bring into subjection every inordinate desire! Every species of life, whether hatched in the egg, formed in the womb, evolved from spawn, produced by metamorphosis, with or without form or intelligence, possessing or devoid of natural instinct — from these changeful[3]

---

[1] Compare the Chinese text of the famous Buddhist tract entitled *Awakening of Faith*, written by *Ma-Ming* (Asvaghocha), "who flourished A.D. 50, under the Indo-Scythic king, Gondophares."

[2] "This work contains the germ of the larger compilation *Prajna-Paramita* in one hundred and twenty volumes. The abstractions of Buddhist philosophy, which were afterwards ramified to such a formidable extent as these numbers indicate, are here found in their primary form, probably as they were taught by Sakyamuni himself."—*Chinese Buddhism.* EDKINS.

[3] Discoursing upon illusory ideas concerning the world of sentient life, the Lord Buddha stated that these were already eliminated from

conditions of being, I command you to seek deliverance,[1] in the transcendental concept of

the minds of his enlightened disciples. The reference in the text is to disciples in process of instruction, and these the Lord Buddha commanded to relegate to oblivion the deceptive idea of the reality of sentient life, to dissolve within their minds its nauseous dregs, to put away its horrid stain, and cause it to vanish like snow in a glowing furnace. —*Chinese Annotation.*

"The very nature of phenomena demonstrates that they must have had a beginning, and that they must have an end."—*Lay Sermons.* HUXLEY.

[1] By adopting the term *Mieh-Tu*, Chinese Buddhists appear well prepared to refute a prevalent notion that their concept of deliverance is equivalent to annihilation. *Mieh* usually means annihilation, but *Tu*—to cross over in safety, is the antithesis of annihilation. After due consideration of the significance of the terminology, perhaps it will be generally conceded that English renderings of *Mieh-Tu* as Deliverance or Salvation, are not without some degree of justification.

"All these I command and exhort to enter on the state of the unsurpassed Nirvana (Pari Nirvana), and for ever to free themselves from the conditions of being to which they severally belong."—*Kin-Kong-King.* BEAL.

Nirvana.[1] Thus, you shall be delivered from an immeasurable, innumerable, and illimitable world of sentient life; but, in reality, there is no world of sentient life from which to seek deliverance. And why? Because, in the minds[2] of enlightened disciples there have

---

[1] "The dewdrop slips into the shining sea."
—*Light of Asia.* Sir EDWIN ARNOLD.
"The dewdrop re-becomes the shining sea."
—*Chioh-Hsien* (a Chinese monk).
"The popular exoteric systems agree in defining Nirvana negatively as a state of absolute exemption from the circle of transmigration as a state of entire freedom from all forms of materiality, from all passion and exertion, mentally and emotionally, a state of indifference therefore alike to joy and pain. Positively they define Nirvana as the highest stage of spiritual liberty and bliss, as absolute immortality through absorption of the soul into itself. Individuality is preserved, and Buddhas who have entered Nirvana occasionally reappear again to intervene on behalf of the faithful."— *Handbook of Chinese Buddhism.* EITEL.

[2] The able commentator *Ti-Ching* observes that many people, like Ananda—a favourite disciple of Buddha—are in error when they suppose their minds to be located within their material bodies. This interesting aspect of

ceased to exist such arbitrary concepts of phenomena as an entity, a being, a living being, or a personality.[1]

Buddhist psychology is made tolerably clear in the familiar narrative known generally as *The Enlightenment of Ananda.* Therein the Lord Buddha endeavours to prove that as objects within ourselves are invisible, the illuminating mind cannot be asserted to inhabit exclusively our material bodies. He also indicates that it cannot be affirmed to occupy any appointed sphere outside ourselves, it being usually understood that we observe only those objects by which we are environed. The Lord Buddha also controverts the theory, enunciated by Ananda, that the mind is secreted somewhere within the organs of sense; which assumption is based upon a notion that the seeing eye, and differentiating mind, are mysteriously correlated.

[1] "This belief in self is regarded so distinctly as a heresy that two well-known words in Buddhist terminology have been coined on purpose to stigmatise it. The first of these is Sakkayaditthi, 'the heresy of individuality,' the name given to this belief as one of the three primary delusions (the others being doubt, and belief in the efficacy of rites or ceremonies) which must be abandoned at the very first stage of the Buddhist path of holiness. The other is Attavada, 'the

THE DIAMOND SUTRA

"Moreover, Subhuti, an enlightened disciple ought to act spontaneously in the exercise of charity,[1] uninfluenced by sensuous phenomena [2]

doctrine of soul or self,' which is the name given to it as a part of the chain of causes which lead to the origin of evil. It is there classed—with sensuality, heresy (as to eternity and annihilation), and belief in the efficacy of rites and ceremonies—as one of the four Upadanas, which are the immediate cause of birth, decay, death, sorrow, lamentation, pain, grief, and despair."—*Buddhism.* T. W. RHYS DAVIDS.

[1] "The first of six Paramita — charity, morality, endurance, energy, contemplation, wisdom—cardinal virtues, or means of progressing towards Nirvana. The virtue of religious charity, implying all kinds of self-denying acts, almsgiving, sacrifice, etc." — *Handbook of Chinese Buddhism.* EITEL.

[2] "The kind of craving excitement, which follows on sensation, and causes the delusion of self and the lust of life—creating either delight in the objects that present themselves, or an eager desire to supply a felt want—this eager yearning thirst growing into sensuality, desire of future life, or love of the present world, is the origin of all suffering. Sorrow and suffering will be overcome, extinguished, if this 'thirst' be quenched, this lust of life destroyed. 'He who overcomes this con-

such as sound, odour, taste, touch, or Law.[1] Subhuti, it is imperative that an enlightened disciple, in the exercise of charity, should act independently of phenomena. And why? Because, acting without regard to illusive forms of phenomena, he will realise in the exercise of charity, a merit inestimable and immeasurable.

---

temptible thirst, sufferings fall off from him like water drops from a lotus leaf.'"—*Buddhism*. T. W. RHYS DAVIDS.

[1] *Fah*, the Chinese equivalent of Dharma—Law, appears to be a generic term for all religious doctrines incidental to Buddhism. The Buddhas are invariably referred to as *Fah-Wang*—Princes of the Law. The Sutras are frequently alluded to as *Fah-Pao*—Jewels of the Law. The monks are usually designated *Fah-Men*—Disciples of the Law. The interminable process of transmigration is depicted by *Fah-Luen*—Wheel of the Law. The dissemination of Buddhistic tenets is typified by *Chuan-Fah-Luen*—Revolving Wheel of the Law. Religious designations consonant with the idea of Law, are held in high esteem amongst the Buddhist ecclesiastical orders. Of such are *Fah-Ai*—Lover of the Law; *Fah-Lien*—Approved in the Law; *Fah-Ming*—Brightness of the Law (compare Eitel's *Handbook of Chinese Buddhism*).

"Subhuti, what think you? Is it possible to estimate the distance comprising the illimitable universe of space?"[1] Subhuti replied, saying: "Honoured of the Worlds! It is impossible to estimate the distance comprising the illimitable universe of space." The Lord Buddha thereupon discoursed, saying: "It is equally impossible to estimate the merit[2] of an enlightened

---

[1] "Subhuti, can the western, or southern, or northern regions of space be measured? or the four midway regions of space (*i.e.*, N.E., S.E., S.W., N.W.), or the upper and lower regions: can either of these be accurately measured or defined?" — *Kin-Kong-King*. BEAL.

[2] "Of all the modes of acquiring merit, that of almsgiving is the principal; it is the chief of the virtues that are requisite for the attainment of the Buddhaship; it is the first of the four great virtues, *viz.*: almsgiving, affability, promoting the prosperity of others, and loving others as ourselves; it is superior to the observance of the precepts—the path that all the Buddhas have trod—a lineage to which they have all belonged. . . . The giving of alms softens the mind, and brings it into subjection, by which the ascetic is prepared for the exercise of the rites he is afterwards to practise. . . . The faithful are required to give

disciple, who discharges the exercise of charity, unperturbed by the seductive influences of phenomena. Subhuti, the mind of an enlightened disciple ought thus to be indoctrinated."[1]

The Lord Buddha interrogated Subhuti, saying: "What think you? Is it possible that by means of his physical body,[2] the Lord

in alms of that which they have honestly earned by their own personal exertions. . . . There must be a willing mind respecting that which they offer, from the time that the intention of making the offering is formed to the time when it is presented, as well as after it has been made. . . . When the gift, the giver, and the receiver are all pure, the reward is proportionately great."—*Eastern Monachism.* SPENCE HARDY.

[1] "Let his livelihood be kindliness,
His conduct righteousness,
Then in the fulness of gladness
He will make an end of grief."
—*Buddhism.* T. W. RHYS DAVIDS.

[2] "Primitive Buddhism distinguished a material, visible, and perishable body (*Seh-Shen—lit.*, the Body of Form) and an immaterial, invisible, immortal body (*Fah-Shen—lit.*, the Body of Law) as the constituents of every personality. This dichotomism, taught, as it

THE DIAMOND SUTRA

Buddha may be clearly perceived?" Subhuti replied, saying: "No! Honoured of the Worlds! It is impossible that by means of his physical body, the Lord Buddha may be clearly perceived. And why? Because, what the Lord Buddha referred to as a physical body, is in reality not merely a physical body." Thereupon the Lord Buddha addressed Subhuti, saying: "Every form or quality of phenomena is transient and illusive. When the mind realises that the phenomena of life are not

seems by Sakyamuni himself, was ever afterwards retained as regards the nature of ordinary mortals. But in later ages, when the combined influence of Sivaism, which ascribed to Siva a threefold body (called *Dharmakaya*—essence, *Sambhogakaya*—reflex intelligence, and *Nirmanakaya*—practical issue of his intelligence), and that of Brahmanism with its Trimurti, gave rise to the Buddhist dogma of a Triratna (*San-Pao*—the precious Buddha, the precious Law, and the precious Priesthood), trichotomism was taught with regard to the nature of all Buddhas. Again they ascribed to every Buddha a triple form of existence, viewing him: (1) as having entered Nirvana; (2) as existing in reflex in the world of form; (3) as existing or having existed on earth."—*Handbook of Chinese Buddhism.* EITEL.

real phenomena, the Lord Buddha may then be clearly perceived."[1]

Subhuti enquired of the Lord Buddha, saying: "Honoured of the Worlds! In future ages, when this scripture is proclaimed, amongst those beings destined to hear, shall any conceive within their minds a sincere, unmingled faith?"[2]

The Lord Buddha replied to Subhuti, saying: "Have no such apprehensive thought! Even at the remote period of five centuries subsequent to the Nirvana of the Lord Buddha,[3] there will

---

[1] The spiritual Buddha must be realised within the mind, otherwise there can be no true perception of the Lord Buddha.—*Chinese Annotation.*

[2] Compare the question addressed by Jesus to His disciples, "When the Son of Man cometh, shall He find faith on the earth?"

[3] "In fulness of the times—it fell
    The Buddha died, the great Tathagata,
    Even as a man 'mongst men, fulfilling all:
    And how a thousand thousand lakhs since then
    Have trod the Path which leads whither he went
    Unto Nirvana, where the Silence lives."
—*The Light of Asia.* SIR EDWIN ARNOLD.

THE DIAMOND SUTRA

be many disciples observing the monastic vows,[1] and assiduously devoted to good works.[2] These, hearing this scripture proclaimed, will believe in its immutability, and similarly conceive within their minds a pure, unmingled faith. Besides, it is important to realise that

---

[1] When a novice seeks admission to a monastic order, an ordination service is conducted by a chapter of monks, at which the following vows are administered. "I take the vow not to destroy life. I take the vow not to steal. I take the vow to abstain from impurity. I take the vow not to lie. I take the vow to abstain from intoxicating drinks, which hinder progress and virtue. I take the vow not to eat at forbidden times. I take the vow to abstain from dancing, singing, music, and stage plays. I take the vow not to use garlands, scents, unguents, or ornaments. I take the vow not to use a high or broad bed. I take the vow not to receive gold or silver." (Compare *Buddhism*. T. W. RHYS DAVIDS.)

[2] "The primary motive for doing good, and worshipping Buddha, according to these scriptures (the Buddha scriptures of Nipal), is the hope of obtaining absorption into the nature of the god, and being freed from transmigrations."—*China*. Sir JOHN FRANCIS DAVIS.

20 THE DIAMOND SUTRA

faith[1] thus conceived, is not exclusively in virtue of the insular thought of any particular Buddha, but because of its affiliation with the concrete[2] thoughts of myriad Buddhas, throughout infinite ages. Therefore, amongst the beings destined to hear this Scripture proclaimed, many, by momentary reflection, will intuitively[3] conceive a pure and holy faith.

[1] "And is thy faith so much to give,
Is it so hard a thing to see,
That the Spirit of God, whate'er it be,
The Law that abides and changes not, ages long,
The Eternal and Nature - Born—these things be strong?"
— *The Bacchae.* EURIPIDES (translated by Gilbert Murray).

[2] "The elements of faith, like the flowers, appear to have their roots in eternity."— *Chang-Ming* (a Chinese monk).

[3] "Were it possible for a Yogi and a Rahat from India, a Greek philosopher from one of the schools holding the power of intuition, an ascetic from the wilds of Syria or the mountains of Egypt, a heretic from the school at Alexandria, a monk from one of the monasteries of Europe, a schoolman of the Middle Ages, and a modern German metaphysician of the school of Schelling to meet

"Subhuti, the Lord Buddha by his prescience,[1] is perfectly cognisant of all such potential disciples, and for these also there is reserved an immeasurable merit. And why? Because, the minds of these disciples will not revert to such arbitrary concepts of phenomena as an

together, and were it possible for them to forget their sectarian subtilties and nice distinctions, they would find that there was a vast mass of speculation about the main principles of which they were agreed. They would be of one mind relative to the four following propositions: (1) That there is an objective potency of intellect; (2) That this potency can be rendered subjective by concentrated thought, ascetic exercises, or determined effort; (3) That this potency can only be acquired by the initiated; (4) That the initiated may enlarge this potency to a limitless extent. As to the efficient cause of the potency, there would be a difference of opinion; some would ascribe it to intuition alone, while others would attribute it to an alliance with higher spirits or with God; but of its existence there would be no doubt."—*Eastern Monachism.* SPENCE HARDY.

[1] "For now I know, by what within me stirs,
   That I shall teach compassion unto men
   And be a speechless world's interpreter."
—*The Light of Asia.* SIR EDWIN ARNOLD.

entity, a being, a living being, a personality, qualities or ideas coincident with Law, or existing apart from the idea of Law. And why? Because, assuming the permanency and reality of phenomena, the minds of these disciples would be involved in such distinctive ideas as an entity, a being, a living being, and a personality. Affirming the permanency and reality of qualities or ideas coincident with Law, their minds would inevitably be involved in resolving these same definitions. Postulating the inviolate nature of qualities or ideas which have an existence apart from the Law, there yet remain to be explained these abstruse distinctions—an entity, a being, a living being, and a personality. Therefore, enlightened disciples ought not to affirm the permanency or reality of qualities or ideas coincident with Law, nor postulate as being of an inviolate nature, qualities or ideas having an existence apart from the concept of Law.

"Thus, we are enabled to appreciate the significance of those words which the Lord Buddha invariably repeated to his followers: 'You disciples must realise that the Law which I enunciated, was presented before your minds in the simile of a raft.[1] If the Law—having fulfilled its function in bearing you to the other shore (Nirvana)[2]—with its coincident qualities and ideas must inevitably be abandoned,[3] how much more inevitable must be the abandonment of qualities or ideas

---

[1] "(By me) is made a well-constructed raft, —so said Bhagavat—I have passed over (to Nibbana), I have reached the further bank, having overcome the torrent (of passions); there is no (further) use for a raft: therefore if thou like, rain, O sky!"—*Sutta-Nipata*. FAUSBÖLL.

[2] Compare an idea expressed by the apostle Paul, "wherefore the law was our schoolmaster to bring us unto Christ." Note, also, the similarity of a metaphor employed in Christian anthology, "We shall meet on that beautiful 'shore.'"

[3] "Our little systems have their day,
　　They have their day and cease to be;
　　They are but broken lights of Thee,
　　But thou, O Lord, art more than they."
　　　　　　　　　—TENNYSON.

"Reposing on eternal truth . . . when thy mind shall have worked through the snares of delusion, then wilt thou attain to indifference to the doctrines, which are either (already) received, or have yet to be received."—*Bhagavad-Gita*. J. COCKBURN THOMSON.

which have an existence apart from the Law?'"

The Lord Buddha addressed Subhuti, saying: "What think you? Has the Lord Buddha really attained to supreme spiritual wisdom? Or has he a system of doctrine which can be specifically formulated?"

Subhuti replied, saying: "As I understand the meaning of the Lord Buddha's discourse, he has no system of doctrine which can be specifically formulated; nor can the Lord Buddha express, in explicit terms, a form of knowledge which can be described as supreme spiritual wisdom. And why? Because, what the Lord Buddha adumbrated in terms of the Law, is transcendental and inexpressible. Being a purely spiritual concept, it is neither consonant with Law, nor synonymous with anything apart from the Law. Thus[1] is exemplified

---

[1] "So it appears that all the sages and wise men who have lived have all adopted this mode of diffusive doctrine [doctrine which admits of no particular distinction (*wou-wei*)], and hence the differences which have occurred."—*Kin-Kong-King.* BEAL.

the manner by which wise disciples and holy Buddhas, regarding intuition[1] as the Law of their minds, severally attained to different planes of spiritual wisdom."[2]

The Lord Buddha addressed Subhuti, saying: "What think you? If a benevolent person bestowed as alms, an abundance of the seven treasures[3] sufficient to fill the universe, would there accrue to that person a considerable merit?"

Subhuti replied, saying:[4] "A very con-

[1] The Chinese text "*i - wu - wei - fah*," is explained by a learned expositor as *tsz-ran-choih-sing*—the intuitive faculty.

[2] "Because that thing which was known or taught by the Tathagata is incomprehensible and inexpressible. It is neither a thing nor no - thing. And why? Because the holy persons are of imperfect power." — *The Vagrakkhedika*. MAX MÜLLER.

[3] Gold, silver, pearls, coral, cornelian, glass, and crystal.

[4] "Very considerable indeed, world-honoured one! But why so? This merit being in its very character of the nature of that which is

siderable merit, Honoured of the Worlds! And why? Because, what is referred to does not partake of the nature of ordinary merit, and in this sense the Lord Buddha made mention of a 'considerable' merit."

The Lord Buddha rejoined, saying: "If a disciple adhered with implicit faith to a stanza[1] of this Scripture, and diligently explained it to others, the intrinsic merit of that disciple would be relatively greater. And why? Because, Subhuti, the holy Buddhas, and the

---

no merit at all, so Tathagata speaks of it as being 'much.'"—*Kin-Kong-King.* BEAL.

"Subhuti said: Yes, O Sugata, that son or daughter of a good family would produce a large stock of merit. And why? Because, O Bhagavat, what was preached by the Tathagata as the stock of merit, is no stock of merit. Therefore, the Tathagata preaches: 'a stock of merit, a stock of merit indeed!'"— *The Vagrakkhedika.* MAX MÜLLER.

[1] "Gatha — hymns and chants, narratives containing moral expositions in metrical language. A Chinese text says, '32 characters form one Gatha,' which refers to a certain variety of Gatha called Aryagiti, a metre consisting of 32 instants."—*Handbook of Chinese Buddhism.* EITEL.

Law[1] by which they attained to supreme spiritual wisdom, severally owe their inception to the truth[2] of this sacred Scripture. Subhuti, what is ordinarily termed the Buddhic Law, is not really a Law attributive to Buddha."[3]

[1] "The *Dharmma* (Law) is perfect, having nothing redundant, and nothing wanting. But it requires attention, that the benefits it offers may be received. Though the teacher may attain great happiness, and enter Nirvana, it does not follow that the disciple will necessarily possess the same privileges; he may be like one who binds the crown upon the head of another. Therefore each one for himself must exercise meditation, and observe the ordinances, that he may attain wisdom." — *Eastern Monachism.* SPENCE HARDY.

[2] "Faith is in the world the best property for a man; *Dhamma* (the Law), well observed, conveys happiness; truth, indeed, is the sweetest of things; and the life they call the best which is lived with understanding."— *Sutta-Nipata.* FAUSBÖLL.

[3] "What then, Subhuti? All the Buddhas, and all the perfect laws of the Buddhas, have sprung from (the principles of) this one Sutra; but, Subhuti, that which is spoken of as the Law of Buddha, is after all not such a Law

The Lord Buddha enquired of Subhuti, saying: "What think you? May a Scrotapatti[1] (having entered the stream which bears on to Nirvana) thus moralise within himself, 'I

(or, is a Law of no Buddha)."—*Kin-Kong-King*. BEAL.

"Because, O Subhuti, the highest perfect knowledge of the holy and enlightened Tathagatas is produced from it; the blessed Buddhas are produced from it. And why? Because, O Subhuti, when the Tathagata preached: 'The qualities of Buddha, the qualities of Buddha indeed!' They were preached by him as no-qualities of Buddha. Therefore they are called the qualities of Buddha." — *The Vagrakkhedika*. MAX MÜLLER.

An erudite Chinese commentator suggests that the words *fei-fuh-fah* are synonymous with *wu-wei-fah*—intuition, already observed in the preceding section. A familiar passage from *Lao-Tsz*, "Infinite truth is inexpressible," is quoted by our commentator as serving to illustrate the difficulty of giving expression to an idea equivalent to the Law of Buddha.

[1] "One who has entered (Apatti) the stream (Srota), the latter being defined as the stream of holy conduct (which bears on to Nirvana)." —*Handbook of Chinese Buddhism*. EITEL.

have obtained the fruits[1] commensurate with the merit of a Scrotapatti'?" Subhuti replied, saying: "No! Honoured of the Worlds! And why? Because, Scrotapatti is simply a descriptive term signifying 'having entered the stream.' A disciple who avoids the seductive phenomena of form, sound, odour, taste, touch, and Law,[2] is named a Scrotapatti."

[1] "Men walking in the path, and standing in the fruits thereof, those who have attained some fruits thereof but are yet learners . . . whose hope is directed to the utmost goal."
— *Questions of King Milinda.* T. W. RHYS DAVIDS.
"Enter the path! There spring the healing streams
Quenching all thirst! there bloom th' immortal flowers
Carpeting all the way with joy! there throng
Swiftest and sweetest hours."
—*The Light of Asia.* Sir EDWIN ARNOLD.

[2] Perhaps in the sense that a Scrotapatti clearly perceives and understands the tentative nature of the Law, his mind being trained to regard it as "a well-constructed raft," designed to bear him safely across the stream of spiritual consciousness upon which he has entered. It also appears that the Scrotapatti discerns in the *idea* of the Law, something as unreal and

The Lord Buddha again enquired of Subhuti, saying: "What think you? May a Sakridagami[1] (who is subject only to one more reincarnation) thus muse within himself, 'I have obtained the fruits consonant with the merit of a Sakridagami'?" Subhuti replied, saying: "No! Honoured of the Worlds! And why? Because, Sakridagami is merely a descriptive title denoting 'only one more reincarnation';[2] but in reality there is no such

ephemeral as the phenomena of form, sound, odour, taste, or touch. In seeking "Nirvana's blest abode," the Scrotapatti endeavours to "rise by daily sojourn with these phantasies —to lovelier verities."

[1] "The path Sakradagami is so called because he who enters it will receive one more birth. He may enter this path in the world of men, and afterwards be born in a Dewa-Loka (a heavenly mansion—in Chinese *Tien-Kong*); or he may enter it in a Dewa-Loka, and afterwards be born in the world of men."—*Eastern Monachism.* SPENCE HARDY.

[2] "Because he is not an individual being (Dharma), who has obtained the state of a Sakridagami."—*The Vagrakkhedika.* MAX MÜLLER.

condition as 'only one more reincarnation,' hence Sakridagami is merely a descriptive title."

The Lord Buddha once again enquired of Subhuti, saying: "What think you? May an Anagami[1] (having entire immunity from reincarnation) thus reflect within himself, 'I have obtained the fruits which accord with the merit of an Anagami?'" Subhuti replied, saying: "No! Honoured of the Worlds! And why? Because, Anagami is merely a designation meaning 'immunity from reincarnation'; but in reality there is no such condition as

---

[1] "Not returning, or not being reborn in the world of desire. The third degree of Buddhistic saintship, the third class of Aryas, embracing all those who are no more liable to be reborn as men, though they are to be born once more as Devas, when they will forthwith become Arhats and enter Nirvana." *Handbook of Chinese Buddhism.* EITEL.

"Men devoid of passion, and of malice, and of dulness, men in whom the great evils (lust, becoming, delusion, and ignorance) are not, men who have neither craving thirst, nor grasping desires."—*Questions of King Milinda.* T. W. RHYS DAVIDS.

'immunity from reincarnation,' hence Anagami is merely a convenient designation."

The Lord Buddha yet again enquired of Subhuti, saying: "What think you? May an Arhat[1] (having attained to absolute quiescence

---

[1] "Explained by *Fuh-Ko* — the Fruit of Buddha (Buddhaphalam). The original meaning of Arhat (deserving, worthy) is overlooked by most Chinese commentators, who explained the term as if it were written *Ari-Hat*—Destroyer of the Enemy. The following two explanations are given, *Shah-Tseh*—Destroying the Enemy, and *Puh-Seng*—not to be reborn, *i.e.*, except from transmigration. There is, however, a third explanation which is based on the original meaning of Arhat, namely *Ying-Kong*—deserving worship. The Arhat is the perfected Arya (one who has mastered the four spiritual truths—*Sz-Ti*—and thereby entered the path to Nirvana called Arya-Marga), and the state of Arhat can accordingly be attained only by passing through the different degrees of saintship. Arhatship implies possession of supernatural powers, and is to be succeeded either by Buddhaship or by immediate entrance into Nirvana."—*Handbook of Chinese Buddhism.* EITEL.

"Those who have entered the stream, and those who, free from stains, will only be of mind) thus meditate within himself, 'I have obtained the condition of an Arhat'?" Subhuti replied, saying: "No! Honoured of the Worlds! And why? Because, there is not in reality a condition synonymous with the term Arhat. Honoured of the Worlds! if an Arhat thus meditates within himself, 'I have obtained the condition of an Arhat,' there would be obvious recurrence of such arbitrary concepts as an entity, a being, a living being, and a personality. Honoured of the Worlds! When the Lord Buddha declared that in absolute quiescence[1] of mind, per-

reborn once more on earth, those who will never again return, and Arhats—these are they who dwell in the 'city of Righteousness.'"—*Questions of King Milinda*. T. W. RHYS DAVIDS.

In the moral philosophy of Mencius there is inculcated a principle of having few desires (*Kwa-Yuh*), and Chinese Buddhists frequently institute comparisons between those "few desires" and "no desires" of the Arhats.

[1] A Chinese annotator suggests it is almost self-evident that "absolute quiescence" is the condition of mind in which knowledge is acquired by intuition.

fect observance of the Law,[1] and true spiritual perception, I was pre-eminent amongst the disciples, I did not cogitate thus within myself, 'I am an Arhat, freed[2] from desire!' Had I thus cogitated, 'I have obtained the

---

[1] " More is the treasure of the Law than gems ;
  Sweeter than comb its sweetness; its delights
  Delightful past compare."
—*The Light of Asia.* Sir EDWIN ARNOLD.

[2] "The man for whom there is nothing upon which he depends, who is independent, having understood the *Dhamma* (Law), for whom there is no desire for coming into existence or having existence—him I call calm. . . . He has overcome desire."—*Dhammapada.* MAX MÜLLER.

"This devotion should be practised with that determination by which thought becomes indifferent (to every worldly object). He who has abandoned all desires which spring from imagination, and has, by means of his heart, kept back the whole collection of the senses from every direction (in which they would go), should gradually become passive by his mind's acquiring firmness, and, by having caused his heart to remain within himself, should not place his thoughts on anything at all."—*Bhagavad-Gita.*—J. COCKBURN THOMSON.

condition of an Arhat,'[1] the 'Honoured of the Worlds' would not have declared concerning me, 'Subhuti delights in the austerities practised by the Aranyaka';[2] but, in reality,

---

[1] "There are some persons who obtain the Rahatship instantaneously, while others can only obtain it by a slow process; they must give alms, make offerings, study the *Bana* (Law), and exercise the necessary discipline."
—*Eastern Monachism.* SPENCE HARDY.

[2] "Explained by 'living in retirement,' 'a hermit,' 'a recluse.' The term signifies ascetics who live in strict seclusion. There are three classes to be distinguished. The first is called *Dharma Aranyaka*—'Hermits of the Law,' their favourite tenet being the doctrine that the principles (*Dharma*) constituting human nature are originally calm, still, and passive. Their favourite tree is the Bodhi tree (tree of intelligence). The second class is called *Matanga Aranyaka*. Its members reside constantly in cemeteries, and are prohibited to approach a village within hearing distance of the lowing of a cow. They are probably called after the Hindoo caste *Matanga*. The third class, or the *Danataka Aranyaka*, is formed by hermits living on the sea beach or on half-tide rocks."
—*Handbook of Chinese Buddhism.* EITEL.

"Men whose home is the forest, men who

Subhuti was perfectly quiescent and oblivious to phenomena;[1] hence the allusion, 'Subhuti

have taken on themselves the extra vows, men full of joy, men who are wearing rough garments, men rejoicing in solitude."—*Questions of King Milinda.* T. W. RHYS DAVIDS.

[1] "The *Sramana* (Buddhist monk) who sets himself to overcome the evils of existence, retires from all intercourse with the world, and either practises meditation, simply, or joins with it the practice of Kasina (an ascetic exercise to free the mind from all agitation), by which he is enabled to attain to *Nimitta* (inward illumination), which is represented as being a mental illumination that brings with it, in various degrees of perfection, the state of mind called *Samadhi* (absolute self-abstraction). This result of profound meditation includes undisturbed tranquillity, and equanimity the most entire, and in its superior degree it produces unconsciousness."—*Eastern Monachism.* SPENCE HARDY.

"The world-honoured one would not then have said: 'Subhuti, what is this but the name of the one who delights in the mortification of an *Aranyaka* (forest devotee),' regarding 'Subhuti' as in truth not acting at all, but as a mere name, then (in such forgetfulness of self) 'he is one who delights in self-mortification.'"—*Kin-Kong-King.* BEAL.

delights in the austerities practised by the Aranyaka.'"

The Lord Buddha addressed Subhuti, saying: "What think you? When the Lord Buddha, in a previous life, was a disciple of Dipankara Buddha,[1] was there communicated

[1] "*Ran-Teng-Fuh*—the Buddha who illuminates brightly, *Ting-Kwang-Fuh*—the Buddha of fixed light. The twenty-fourth predecessor of Sakyamuni, from whom the latter received the assurance of his being destined for Buddhaship."—*Handbook of Chinese Buddhism.* EITEL.

It is recorded in *The Diamond Sutra* that the Lord Buddha, in previous incarnations, assiduously performed religious vows, and deferentially honoured all contemporary Buddhas. An image of a former master, Dipankara Buddha, may frequently be observed in Chinese Buddhist temples, immediately behind the more conspicuous figure of Sakyamuni Buddha. Amongst Chinese Buddhist anniversaries may be found the birthday of "the ancient Buddha, *Ran-Teng*" (Dipankara), and the period allocated for its observance is the 22nd day of the 8th month. (Compare Edkins' *Chinese Buddhism*.)

to him any prescribed Law, or system of doctrine, whereby he eventually became a Buddha?" Subhuti replied, saying: "No! Honoured of the Worlds! When the Lord Buddha was a disciple of Dipankara Buddha, neither prescribed Law nor system of doctrine was communicated to him, whereby he eventually became a Buddha."[1]

The Lord Buddha addressed Subhuti, saying: "What think you? may an enlightened disciple thus ponder within himself, 'I shall create numerous Buddhist Kingdoms'?"[2]

---

[1] "It is maintained by the Buddhists that the founder of their faith was entirely αὐτοδιδακτος. The wisdom that he manifested was the outbeaming of a self-enkindled flame, not an inspiration from any exterior source, nor was it the result of any process of thought or reason. To whatever object he directed his intellectual vision, whether it was near or remote, whether past, present, or future, he saw it in a moment, intuitively, and yet in a manner the most absolutely perfect." — *Eastern Monachism.* SPENCE HARDY.

[2] "Bhagavat said: If Subhuti, a Bodhisattva, should say, 'I shall create numbers of worlds,' he would say what is untrue. And why? Because, O Subhuti, when Tathagata preached

Subhuti replied, saying: "No! Honoured of the Worlds! And why? Because, kingdoms numbers of worlds, numbers of worlds indeed! they were preached by him as no numbers. Therefore they are called numbers of worlds."—*The Vagrakkhedika.* MAX MÜLLER.

"Subhuti, what think you? are the various lands and territories of the Buddhas completely perfected by the Bodhisatwas who occupy them? No! World-honoured one! for this complete perfection of which we speak is after all no perfection at all, it is only an empty name."—*Kin-Kong-King.* BEAL.

"The wise man is always thinking: How can I and these beings become Buddhas? I will preach this true Law, upon which the happiness of all beings depends, for the benefit of the world."—*Saddharma-Pundarika.* H. KERN.

The words *Chuang-Yen*, in a Buddhist sense, usually refer to the erection or adornment of temples and pagodas, almsgiving, or other work of merit. Used in conjunction with *Fuh-Tu*—Buddhist kingdoms, as exemplified by our text, *Chuang-Yen* appears to convey a much wider meaning. Perhaps it refers to a spiritual creation and adornment by charity and virtue, of kingdoms owning allegiance to the Lord Buddha.

"In twelve years from the commencement of his public teaching, Buddha's doctrines had spread over sixteen Indian kingdoms."—*Chinese Buddhism.* EDKINS.

thus created would not in reality be Buddhist kingdoms,[1] therefore 'the creation of numerous Buddhist kingdoms' is merely a figure of speech."

The Lord Buddha, continuing, addressed Subhuti, saying: "Enlightened disciples ought therefore to engender within themselves a pure and holy mind; they ought not to depend on the phenomena of form, sound, odour, taste, touch, or Law; they ought to sedulously cultivate a mind independent of every material aid."

The Lord Buddha addressed Subhuti, saying: "Supposing a man with a body as pretentious as Sumeru,[2] prince among moun-

---

[1] A Buddhist kingdom has no outward manifestation; it is a pure and holy condition of mind.—*Chinese Annotation.*

Compare the statement attributed to Christ, "The kingdom of heaven is *within* you."

[2] "Sumeru is probably Elburz, an isolated mountain of the Caucasus range, 18,000 feet in height, and surrounded by low ground."—*Chinese Buddhism.* EDKINS.

"But when they brought the painted palanquin
 To fetch him home, the bearers of the poles
 Were the four Regents of the Earth, come down
 From Mount Sumeru."

—*The Light of Asia.* Sir EDWIN ARNOLD.

tains, would you esteem such a body as being great?" Subhuti replied, saying: "Exceedingly great, Honoured of the Worlds! And why? Because, the Lord Buddha referred not to a physical body,[1] but to mental and

[1] "The modification which Buddhism introduced into the idea of transmigration was necessitated by the early Buddhist theories of the nature of sentient beings; according to which, man consists of an assemblage of different properties or qualities . . . these are Material qualities, Sensations, abstract Ideas, Tendencies of mind, and mental Powers . . . The first group, Material Qualities, are like a mass of foam, that gradually forms, and then vanishes. The second group, the Sensations, are like a bubble dancing on the face of the water. The third group, the Ideas, are like the uncertain mirage that appears in the sunshine. The fourth group, the mental and moral Predispositions, are like the plantain stalk, without firmness or solidity. And the last group, the Thoughts, are like a spectre or magical illusion. The body itself is constantly changing, . . . man is never the same for two consecutive moments." (Compare Rhys Davids' *Buddhism*, and Spence Hardy's *Manual*.)

"For instance, Subhuti, a man might have a body and a large body, so that his size should be as large as the king of mountains, spiritual concepts of bodies, in which sense a body may be regarded as really Great.

The Lord Buddha addressed Subhuti, saying: "If there were rivers Ganges as numerous as the sands of the Ganges, would the aggregate grains of sand[1] be of considerable number?" Subhuti replied, saying: "Of very considerable number, Honoured of the Worlds! The rivers Ganges alone would be innumerable, and much more innumerable would be the grains of sand."

The Lord Buddha thereupon addressed Subhuti, saying: "I have a truth to declare

Sumeru. Do you think then, O Subhuti, that his selfhood would be large? Subhuti said, Yes! his selfhood would be large. And why? Because, when the Tathagata preached 'selfhood,' selfhood indeed! it was preached by him as no selfhood. Therefore it is called selfhood."—*The Vagrakkhedika.* MAX MÜLLER.

[1] "Sarvanikchepa, by which you deal
 With all the sands of Gunga, till we come
 To Antah-Kalpas, where the unit is
 The sands of ten crore Gungas."

—*The Light of Asia.* Sir EDWIN ARNOLD.

unto you! If a good disciple, whether man or woman, were to bestow in the exercise of charity, an abundance of the seven treasures,[1] sufficient to fill as many boundless universes as there would be grains of sand in these innumerable rivers, would the cumulative merit of such a disciple be considerable?" Subhuti replied, saying: "Very considerable, Honoured of the Worlds!"

The Lord Buddha then declared unto Subhuti, "If a good disciple, whether man or woman, were with implicit faith to adhere to a stanza of this Scripture, and diligently explain it to others, the consequent merit would be relatively greater than the other."

The Lord Buddha, continuing, said unto Subhuti: "Wherever this Scripture is proclaimed, even though it were but a stanza

[1] Gold, silver, pearls, coral, cornelian, glass, and crystal.
"As much of the seven precious substances as would fill as many great chiliocosms as there are sands in all the rivers above described."—*Kin-Kong-King*. BEAL.

comprising four lines, you should realise that that place would be sanctified by the presence of the whole realm of gods, men, and terrestrial spirits,[1] who ought unitedly to worship, as if before a sacred shrine of Buddha.[2] But what encomium shall express the merit of a disciple who rigorously observes, and diligently studies,[3] the text of

[1] Adopting Max Müller's rendering. In the Chinese text are *Tien*, *Ren*, and *O-Siu-Lo*—heaven, or gods—men, and *Asurus*; the latter defined as *fei-tien*—not celestial spirits.

[2] "Whatever spirits have come together here, either belonging to the earth or living in the air, let us worship the perfect Buddha, revered by gods and men.

"Whatever spirits have come together here, either belonging to the earth or living in the air, let us worship the perfect *Dhamma* (Law), revered by gods and men.

"Whatever spirits have come together here, either belonging to the earth or living in the air, let us worship the perfect *Sangha* (community of monks), revered by gods and men."—*Dhammapada.* MAX MÜLLER.

[3] "Earnestness is the path of immortality (Nirvana), thoughtlessness the path of death. Those who are in earnest do not die, those who are thoughtless are as if dead already."—*Dhammapada.* MAX MÜLLER.

THE DIAMOND SUTRA

this Scripture? Subhuti, you should realise that such a disciple will be endowed[1] with spiritual powers commensurate with initiation in the supreme, incomparable, and most wonderful Law.[2] Whatever place constitutes

[1] "They, O Subhuti, will be endowed with the highest wonder (with what excites the highest wonder). And in that place, O Subhuti, there dwells the teacher (Sasa, often the name of Buddha), or one after another holding the place of the wise preceptor. (This may refer to a succession of teachers handing down the tradition one to another.)"
—*The Vagrakkhedika*. MAX MÜLLER.

"Subhuti, know that this man has acquired knowledge of the most excellent and desirable of all Laws; and if the place where this Sutra is recited be worthy of all honour as the place of Buddha himself, so also is this disciple honourable and worthy of the highest respect."
—*Kin-Kong-King*. BEAL.

[2] "The praises of the *Bana* (Law) are a favourite subject with the native authors. . . . The discourses of Buddha are as a divine charm to cure the poison of evil desire; a divine medicine to heal the disease of anger; a lamp in the midst of the darkness of ignorance; a fire, like that which burns at the end of a Kalpa, to destroy the evils of repeated existence; a meridian sun to dry

a repository for this sacred Scripture, there also the Lord Buddha may be found, together with disciples worthy of reverence and honour."

Upon that occasion, Subhuti enquired of the Lord Buddha, saying: "Honoured of the Worlds! by what name shall this Scripture be known, that we may regard it with reverence?" The Lord Buddha replied, saying: "Subhuti, this Scripture shall be

up the mud of covetousness; a great rain to quench the flame of sensuality; a thicket to block up the road that leads to the *Narakas* (place of the wicked); a ship in which to sail to the opposite shore of the ocean of existence; a collyrium for taking away the eye-film of heresy; a moon to bring out the night-blowing lotus of merit; a succession of trees bearing immortal fruit, placed here and there, by which the traveller may be enabled to cross the desert of existence; . . . a straight highway by which to pass to the incomparable wisdom; a door of entrance to the eternal city of Nirvana; . . . a treasury of the best things it is possible to obtain; and a power by which may be appeased the sorrow of every sentient being."—*Eastern Monachism*. SPENCE HARDY.

known as *The Diamond Sutra*,[1] 'The Transcendent Wisdom,' by means of which we reach 'The Other Shore.' By this name you shall reverently regard it! And why? Subhuti, what the Lord Buddha declared as 'transcendent wisdom' by means of which we reach 'the other shore,' is not essentially 'transcendent wisdom' —in its essence it transcends all wisdom."

The Lord Buddha addressed Subhuti, saying:[2] "What think you? Did the Lord

---

[1] A Chinese annotator observes, that as the "diamond" excels all other precious gems in brilliance and indestructibility, so also the "wisdom" of this Sutra transcends and shall outlive all other knowledge known to philosophy.

[2] "Then what do you think, O Subhuti, is there anything that was preached by the Tathagata? Subhuti said: Not indeed, O Bhagavat, there is nothing that was preached by the Tathagata."—*The Vagrakkhedika.* MAX MÜLLER.

It appears to be one of the distinctive features of primitive Buddhism, that its founder made provision for the utmost development of the human intellect, within the spheres of religion and philosophy. According to the text of *The Diamond Sutra*, the Lord Buddha evidently disclaims any suggestion on his part to formulate a "precise system of Law or doctrine" corresponding to the idea of a *creed*.

Buddha formulate a precise system of Law or doctrine?" Subhuti replied, saying: "Honoured of the Worlds! The Lord Buddha did not formulate a precise system of Law or doctrine."

The Lord Buddha addressed Subhuti, saying: "What think you? within the myriad worlds which comprise this universe, are the atoms of dust numerous?"[1] Subhuti replied, saying: "Very numerous, Honoured of the Worlds!"

---

[1] "Matter is infinitely divisible."—*The World as Idea and Will.* SCHOPENHAUER.

"After me repeat
Your numeration . . . .
By Pundarikas unto Padumas,
Which last is how you count the utmost grains
Of Hastagiri ground to finest dust."
—*The Light of Asia.* Sir EDWIN ARNOLD.

"If the Buddha was not a materialist, in the sense of believing in the eternal existence of material atoms, neither could he in any sense be called a 'spiritualist,' or believer in the external existence of abstract spirit. With him creation did not proceed from an omnipotent spirit or mind evolving phenomena out of itself by the exercise of will, nor from an eternal self-existing, self-evolving germ of any kind. As to the existence in the universe of any spiritual substance which was not matter and

THE DIAMOND SUTRA

The Lord Buddha continuing his discourse, said: "Subhuti, the Lord Buddha declares that all these 'atoms of dust' are not essentially 'atoms of dust,' they are merely termed 'atoms of dust.' The Lord Buddha also declares that those 'myriad worlds' are not really 'myriad worlds,' they are merely designated 'myriad worlds.'"

The Lord Buddha addressed Subhuti, saying: "What think you? Can the Lord Buddha be perceived by means of his thirty-two bodily distinctions?"[1] Subhuti replied, saying: "No! Honoured of the Worlds! the Lord Buddha cannot be perceived by means of his thirty-

---

was imperceptible to the senses, it could not be proved." — *Buddhism.* Sir MONIER WILLIAMS.

"Subhuti, all these countless particles of dust Tathagata declares are no real particles; it is but an empty name by which they are known. Tathagata declares that all these systems of worlds composing the great chiliocosm are no real worlds; they are but empty names."—*Kin-Kong-King.* BEAL.

[1] "Characteristic physiological marks by which every Buddha may be recognised."—*Handbook of Chinese Buddhism.* EITEL.

"Can Tathagata be known by the thirty-two bodily distinctions. And why? Because, what the Lord Buddha referred to as his 'thirty-two bodily distinctions,' are not in reality 'bodily distinctions,' they are merely defined as 'bodily distinctions.'"

The Lord Buddha addressed Subhuti, saying:

two signs (of a hero)?"—*The Vagrakkhedika.* MAX MÜLLER.

"The King saluted, and Queen Maya made
 To lay her babe before such holy feet;
 But when he saw the prince the old man cried
 'Ah, Queen not so!' and thereupon he touched
 Eight times the dust, laid his waste visage there,
 Saying, 'O Babe! I worship! Thou art He!
 I see the rosy light, the foot-sole marks,
 The soft curled tendrils of the Swastika,
 The sacred primal signs thirty-and-two,
 The eighty lesser tokens. Thou art Buddh,
 And thou wilt preach the Law and save all flesh
 Who learn the Law."
—*The Light of Asia.* Sir EDWIN ARNOLD.

"Bright were the divine lineaments of his face, and as the Master (of the Law) gazed in awe and holy reverence, he knew not how to compare the spectacle; the body of Buddha and his Kashaya robe were of a yellowish red colour, and from his knees upward the distinguishing marks of his person were exceedingly glorious."—*The Life of Hiuen-Tsang.* BEAL.

"If a good disciple, whether man or woman, day by day sacrificed lives innumerable as the sands of the Ganges;[1] and if another disciple adhered with implicit faith to a stanza of this Scripture, and diligently explained it to others, the intrinsic merit of such a disciple would be relatively greater than the other."[2]

Upon that occasion, the venerable Subhuti, hearing the text of this scripture proclaimed,

[1] The Chinese expression *Shen - Ming*—life, invariably refers to life in an ordinary material sense, and which may be offered in sacrifice. But in Buddhist philosophy there is a spiritual *Atman*, which can be disposed of only by knowledge.

[2] "Were any one to fill the bowl of Buddha with the choicest food, or to present oil, sugar, honey, medicaments in the greatest abundance, or to build thousands of *Wiharas* (monasteries or temples) splendid as those of Anuradhapura (an ancient city in Ceylon, the Anurogrammum of Ptolemy), or to present an offering to Buddha like that of Anepidu (a rich merchant of Sewet), the hearing or reading of one stanza of the *Bana* (Law) would be more meritorious than all."—*Eastern Monachism.* SPENCE HARDY.

and profoundly realising its meaning, was moved to tears. Addressing the Lord Buddha, he said: "Thou art of transcendent wisdom, Honoured of the Worlds! The Lord Buddha in expounding this supreme canon of Scripture, surpassed in perspicuity every exposition previously heard by me, since my eyes[1] were privileged to perceive this most excellent wisdom. Honoured of the Worlds! in years to come, if disciples hearing this scripture proclaimed, and having within their minds a pure and holy faith, engender true concepts of the ephemeral nature of phenomena— we ought to realise that the cumulative merit of such disciples will be intrinsic and wonderful. Honoured of the Worlds! The true concept of phenomena is, that these are not essentially phenomena, and hence the

---

[1] "As one raises what has been overthrown, or reveals what has been hidden, or tells the way to him who has gone astray, or holds out an oil lamp in the dark that those who have eyes may see the objects, even so by the venerable Gotama in manifold ways the *Dhamma* (Law) has been illustrated."— *Dhammapada*. MAX MÜLLER.

THE DIAMOND SUTRA 53

Lord Buddha declared that they are merely termed phenomena."

"Honoured of the Worlds! having heard this unprecedented Scripture, faith, clear understanding, and firm resolve to observe its precepts, follow as a natural sequence. If, in future ages, disciples destined to hear this Scripture, likewise believe, understand, and observe its precepts, their merit will incite the highest wonder and praise.[1] And why? Because, the minds of those disciples[2] will have outgrown such arbitrary ideas of phenomena

---

[1] "The chief of the priests of that establishment (the Jayendra convent) was a man of high moral character. He observed with the greatest strictness the religious rules and ordinances. He was possessed of the highest intelligence, and acquainted with all the points of a true disciple. His talents were eminent; his spiritual powers exalted; and his disposition affectionate."—*The Life of Hiuen-Tsang.* BEAL.

[2] "They had within themselves the possession of a power by which all objective truth could be presented to their intellectual vision. They, therefore, partook of what in other systems would be regarded as divinity."—*Eastern Monachism.* SPENCE HARDY.

as an entity, a being, a living being, or a personality. And why? Because, the entity is in reality non-entity; and a being, a living being, or a personality, are ideas equally nebulous and hypothetical.[1] Wherefore, discarding every arbitrary idea of phenomena, the wise and wholly enlightened were severally designated Buddha."[2]

The Lord Buddha, assenting, said unto Subhuti: "If, in future ages, disciples destined to hear this Scripture, neither become perturbed

---

[1] "They have been divided into existing and non-existing, real and unreal, by those who had wrong notions; other laws also, of permanency, of being produced, of birth from something already produced, are wrongly assumed." — *Saddharma - Pundarika.* H. KERN.

[2] "But, O Bhagavat, there will not arise in them any idea of a self, of a being, of a living being, of a person, nor does there exist for them any idea of no-idea. And why? Because, the idea of a self is no-idea, the idea of a being is no-idea, the idea of a living being is no-idea, the idea of a person is no-idea. And why? Because, the blessed Buddhas are freed from all ideas." — *The Vagrakkhedika.* MAX MÜLLER.

by its extreme modes of thought,[1] nor alarmed by its lofty sentiments,[2] nor apprehensive about realising its high ideals[3]—these disciples also, by their intrinsic merit, will incite superlative wonder and praise."

"Subhuti, what the Lord Buddha referred to as the first *Paramita*[4] (charity), is not in reality

[1] . . . . "For birth and death
End hence for me and those who learn my Law."
—*The Light of Asia*—Sir EDWIN ARNOLD.

[2] "As the Buddhist strove to reach a state of quietism or holy meditation in this world, namely the state of the perfect disciple or Arhat; so he looked forward to an eternal calm in the world to come, Nirvana. Buddha taught that this end could only be attained by the practice of virtue."—*The Indian Empire*. Sir WILLIAM HUNTER.

[3] "The heart of it is love, the end of it
Is peace and consummation sweet."
—*The Light of Asia*. Sir EDWIN ARNOLD.

[4] The first of six *Paramita*—charity, morality, endurance, energy, contemplation, wisdom—or means of attaining to Nirvana.

"What the Tathagata preaches as the *Prajna-Paramita*, that was preached also by innumerable Blessed Buddhas. Therefore it is called the *Prajna-Paramita*."—*The Vagrakkhedika*. MAX MÜLLER.

the first *Paramita*, it is merely termed the first *Paramita*."

"Subhuti, regarding the third *Paramita* (endurance), it is not in reality a *Paramita*, it is merely termed a *Paramita*. And why? Because, in a previous life, when the Prince of Kalinga[1] ('Kaliradja') severed the flesh

---

[1] "An ancient kingdom S.E. of Kos'ala, a nursery of heretical sects, the present Calingapatah, a town in the northern Circars (Lat. 18° 15 N., Long. 85° 11 E.)."—*Handbook of Chinese Buddhism.* EITEL.

It is recorded that the Lord Buddha, in a previous incarnation, was living in a mountainous region, strictly observing the monastic vows. The Prince of Kalinga, a cruel and dissolute ruler, having organised a hunting expedition, visited the secluded region, accompanied by numerous ladies of his harem. Fatigued by the excitement of the chase, the prince fell into a deep siesta. Meantime, the ladies resolved upon a short excursion along a mountain path. Unexpectedly meeting the Lord Buddha, they were greatly astonished at his dignified bearing and edifying conversation. When the prince awoke from his siesta, he was irritated to find that his ladies had disappeared. Instituting an immediate search, he became filled with implacable rage upon from my limbs and body, at that time I was oblivious to such arbitrary ideas of phenomena as an entity, a being, a living being, or a personality. And why? Because, upon that occasion, when my limbs and body were rent asunder, had I not been oblivious to such arbitrary ideas as an entity, a being, a living being, or a personality, there would have originated within my mind, feelings of anger and resentment."

"Subhuti, five hundred incarnations ago,[1]

discovering them in the society of a hermit. The incident, as narrated in the Chinese text, proved to be a distressing sequel to the modest ladies' innocent adventure. (Compare *Chinese Annotations*, etc.)

[1] "Various forms of pre-existence to the number of 500 or 550 are recorded, in the course of which he (Buddha) marked his way up through as many different stages of transmigration from the lowest spheres of life to the highest, practising all kinds of asceticism, and exhibiting in every form the utmost unselfishness and charity." — *Handbook of Chinese Buddhism.* EITEL.

"I and thou, O Arjuna! have passed through many transmigrations. I know all these. . . . Even though I am unborn, of changeless essence, and the lord also of all which exist, yet, in presiding over nature (Prakrita), which

I recollect that as a recluse practising the ordinances of the Kshanti-Paramita,[1] even then I had no such arbitrary ideas as an entity, a being, a living being, or a personality. Therefore, Subhuti, an enlightened disciple ought to discard as being unreal and illusive, every conceivable form of phenomena.[2] In aspiring

is mine, I am born by my own mystic power (Maya). For whenever there is a relaxation of duty, . . . and an increase of impiety, I then reproduce myself for the protection of the good. . . . I am produced in every age."
—*Bhagavad-Gita.* J. COCKBURN THOMSON.

[1] "Explained by patient endurance of insult. The virtue of patience, implying constant equanimity under persecution, and excluding hatred and revenge."—*Handbook of Chinese Buddhism.* EITEL.

"Because, O Subhuti, I remember the past five hundred births, when I was the *Rishi-Kshantivadin* (preacher of endurance)."—*The Vagrakkhedika.* MAX MÜLLER.

[2] "Let (the Bodhisattva) be concentrated in mind, attentive, ever firm as the peak of Mount Sumeru, and in such a state (of mind) look upon all laws (and things) as having the nature of space (as being void), permanently equal to space, without essence, immovable, without substantiality. These, indeed, are the Laws, all and for ever."—*Saddharma-Pundarika.* H. KERN.

to supreme spiritual wisdom, the mind ought to be insensible to every sensuous influence, and independent of everything pertaining to sound, odour, taste, touch, or Law. There ought to be cultivated a condition of complete independence of mind; because, if the mind is depending upon any external aid, it is obviously deluded—there is in reality nothing external to depend upon.[1] Therefore, the Lord Buddha declared that in the exercise of charity, the mind of an enlightened disciple ought not to depend upon any form of phenomena. Subhuti, an enlightened disciple desirous to confer benefits upon the whole realm of being, ought thus to be animated in the exercise of charity."[2]

[1] "Because what is believed is not believed (not to be depended on)."—*The Vagrakkhedika.* MAX MÜLLER.

[2] "Hence Buddha declares that the mind of a Bodhisatwa ought not to rely on any formal act of charity. Subhuti, the Bodhisatwa ought to distribute his almsgiving for the purpose of benefiting the whole mass of sentient creatures, and yet Tathagata declares that as all dependencies are after all no real subjects of dependence, so also he says that all sentient creatures are not in reality what they are called."—*Kin-Kong-King.* BEAL.

The Lord Buddha, in declaring the "unreality of phenomena," also affirmed "that the whole realm of sentient life is ephemeral and illusory."[1]

"Subhuti, the sayings of the Lord Buddha are true, credible, and immutable. His utterances are neither extravagant nor chimerical. Subhuti, the plane[2] of thought to which the Lord Buddha attained, cannot be explained in terms synonymous with reality or non-reality."

"Subhuti, in the exercise of charity, if the mind of an enlightened disciple is not independent of every Law, he is like unto a person having entered impenetrable darkness, and to whom every object is invisible. But an enlightened disciple, discharging the exercise of charity with a mind independent of every Law, is like unto a person having the power of vision, in the meridian glory of the sunlight, and to whom every object is visible."

"Subhuti, in future ages, if a good disciple, whether man or woman, rigorously studies and

---

[1] Literally, "Every form of phenomena is really *not* phenomena; every form of sentient life is in reality *not* sentient life."
[2] The Buddhist term, *Fah* (Law).

observes the text of this Scripture; the Lord Buddha, by means of his Buddhic wisdom,[1] entirely knows and perceives that for such a disciple there is reserved a cumulative merit, immeasurable and illimitable."

The Lord Buddha addressed Subhuti, saying: "If a good disciple, whether man or woman, in the morning, at noonday, and at eventide, sacrificed lives innumerable as the sands of the Ganges, and thus without intermission

[1] "The omniscience of Buddha is not the knowledge of all things, but the power of knowing whatever he wishes to know. In opposition to other teachers, who deduce their doctrines from certain previously assumed principles, and who may err either in the data, or in the deductions from them. Buddha affirms of himself that the complete field of truth is before him, that the eye of wisdom to perceive it was obtained by him when he became a Buddha; and whatever he desires to know he perceives perfectly, and at one glance, without any reasoning process."—(Rev. D. T. Gogerly, in the *Ceylon Friend*. Quoted by R. Spence Hardy, in *Eastern Monachism*).

throughout infinite ages; and if another disciple, hearing this Scripture proclaimed, steadfastly believed it, his felicity would be appreciably greater than the other. But how much greater must be the felicity of a disciple who transcribes the sacred text, observes its precepts, studies its Laws, and repeats the Scripture that others may be edified thereby?"

"Subhuti, the relative importance of this Scripture may thus be summarily stated: its truth is infinite; its worth incomparable; and its merit interminable."

"The Lord Buddha delivered this Scripture specifically for those who are entered upon the path which leads to Nirvana, and for those who are attaining to the ultimate plane of Buddhic thought.[1] If a disciple rigorously

---

[1] Literally, for the *ta-cheng-che* — those of the great vehicle, *i.e.*, the Mahayana faith. "They taught (the Mahayana school) that there were two methods of salvation, or, so to speak, two ways or two vehicles—the great and the little (Maha-Yana and Hina-Yana)— and indeed two Bodhis or forms of true knowledge which these vehicles had to convey (there was also a middle way). The former was for ordinary persons, the latter

observes, studies, and widely disseminates the knowledge of this Scripture, the Lord Buddha entirely knows and perceives that for such an one there will be a cumulative merit, immeasurable, incomparable, illimitable, and inconceivable. All such disciples will be endowed with transcendent Buddhic wisdom and enlightenment.[1] And why? Because, Subhuti, if a disciple takes pleasure in a

for beings of larger talents and higher spiritual powers."—*Buddhism.* Sir MONIER WILLIAMS.

"Therefore let one always be thoughtful, and avoid (gross) pleasures; having abandoned them, let him cross the stream, after baling out the ship, and go to the other shore (Nirvana)."—*Dhammapada.* MAX MÜLLER.

[1] "All these beings will equally remember the *Bodhi* (the highest Buddhic knowledge), will receive it and understand it." — *The Vagrakkhedika.* MAX MÜLLER.

"All men being one with *ho-tan* (Gautama?) Tathagata, arrive at the state of the unsurpassed, just, and enlightened (heart)."—*Kin-Kong-King.* BEAL.

The Chinese phrase "*ho-tan-Ju-Lai,*" may mean to bear upon the person evidences of the Lord Buddha. Compare the statement of the apostle Paul, "I bear in my body evidences of the Lord Jesus Christ."

narrow or exclusive form of the Law,[1] he cannot receive with gratification[2] the instruction of this Scripture, or delight in its study, or fervently explain it to others. Subhuti, in whatever place there is a repository for this Scripture, the whole realm of spiritual beings ought to adore it; and reverencing it as a sacred shrine,[3] ceremoniously surround

---

[1] Those disciples associated with the *Siao-Fah* (little Law, the Hinayana school of Buddhist thought), are rather ungraciously referred to by a Chinese commentator as "rootless stems"; by which we are reminded of the Hindoo aphorism, "from the absence of a root within the root, all things are rootless."

[2] When the Lord Buddha delivered the Sutra known as the *Lotus of the Good Law*, it is recorded that five thousand followers forsook him, owing to what they regarded as a grave difficulty in complying with its intensely abstruse doctrines.

[3] "In these two places also Topes (where relics of Buddha are deposited and safeguarded) have been built, both adorned with layers of all the previous substances (gold, silver, pearls, coral, cornelian, glass, and crystal). The kings, ministers, and peoples of the kingdoms vie with one another in making offerings at them. The trains of those who come to scatter flowers

it, scattering profusely sweet-scented flowers, and pure odours of fragrant incense."[1]

The Lord Buddha, continuing, addressed Subhuti, saying: "If a good disciple, whether man or woman, devoted to the observance and study of this Scripture, is thereby despised,

and light lamps at them never cease."—*The Travels of Fa-Hien.* LEGGE.

This descriptive scene concerning the endless trains of pilgrims who lit their lamps at the sacred shrine, may recall to our minds the beautifully expressed line in Sophocles' *Œdipus Coloneus*, thus rendered by Professor Jebb, *The torch-lit strand* of Eleusis.

[1] Then the king, with his assembled ministers and all the priests belonging to the capital (of Kasmir), advanced to the preaching hall (*Dharmasala*), and escorted him (the Master of the Law) onwards, being altogether something like a thousand men, with standards and parasols, with incense and flowers filling the roads. When they met (the Master of the Law) they all performed a humble salutation, and spread before him countless flowers as religious offerings."—*The Life of Hiuen-Tsang.* BEAL.

or lightly esteemed,[1] it is because that in a previous life there had been committed some grievous transgression, followed now by inexorable retribution.[2] But, although in this life despised or lightly esteemed, the compensating merit thus acquired will cause the transgression of a former life to be fully expiated, and the disciple adequately recompensed

---

[1] "Whoever reviles Buddha or his disciple, be he a wandering mendicant, or a householder, let one know him as an outcast." — *Sutta-Nipata.* V. FAUSBÖLL.

[2] "Whatever evil deeds these beings have done in a former birth, deeds that must lead to suffering, those deeds these beings, owing to their being overcome, after they have seen the Law, will destroy, and they will obtain the knowledge of Buddha."—*The Vagrakkhedika.* MAX MÜLLER.

"According to the Buddha . . . all men must suffer in their own persons either in the present life, or in future lives, the consequences of their own acts. . . . The penalty of sin could not be transferred to another—it could only be borne by the sinner himself, just as the reward of virtue could only be enjoyed by the virtuous man himself."—*Hinduism.* Sir MONIER WILLIAMS.

by the attainment of supreme spiritual wisdom."

"Furthermore, Subhuti, numberless ages ago, I recollect that before the advent of Dipankara Buddha, there were myriad Buddhas before whom I served and received religious instruction, my conduct being entirely blameless and without reproach. But, in the ages to come, if a disciple be enabled to rigorously observe and to study the text of this Scripture, the merit thus acquired will so far exceed the measure of my merit in the service of those myriad Buddhas, that it cannot be stated in terms of proportion, nor comprehended by means of any 'analogy.'"

"Again, Subhuti, in future ages, if a good disciple, whether man or woman, be enabled to rigorously observe and to study consecutively the texts of this Scripture, were I to elaborate either the nature or extent of this merit, those who heard it might become delirious, or entirely doubt its credibility.[1] Subhuti, it is necessary to realise, that as the meaning of this Scripture is beyond ordinary comprehension,

[1] Literally, "become as doubtful as a fox."

the scope of its fruitful rewards is equally incomprehensible."[1]

Upon that occasion, the venerable Subhuti addressed the Lord Buddha, saying: "Honoured of the Worlds! if a good disciple, whether man or woman, having desired to attain to supreme spiritual wisdom, what immutable Law shall support the mind of that disciple, and bring into subjection every inordinate desire?"[2]

[1] "For as the method and entire meaning of this Sutra is not to be described or entirely conceived, so the merit and happy consequences of accepting it cannot be conceived or described."—*Kin-Kong-King*. BEAL.

[2] "Let a man restraining all these remain in devotion. . . . For he, whose senses are under his control, possesses spiritual knowledge. Attachments to objects of sense arise in a man who meditates upon them; from attachment arises desire; from desire passion springs up; from passion comes bewilderment; from bewilderment, confusion of the memory; from confusion of the memory, destruction of the intellect; from destruction of the intellect, he perishes." — *Bhagavad-Gita*. J. COCKBURN THOMSON.

THE DIAMOND SUTRA

The Lord Buddha replied, saying: "A good disciple, whether man or woman, ought thus to habituate his mind:[1] 'I must become oblivious to every idea of sentient life; and having become oblivious to every idea of sentient life, there is *no one* to whom the idea of sentient life has become oblivious.'[2] And why? Because,

---

[1] "He should thus frame his thought: all things must be delivered by me in the perfect world of Nirvana. . . . And why? Because, O Subhuti, there is no such thing as one who has entered on the path of the Bodhisattva."
—*The Vagrakkhedika.* MAX MÜLLER.

[2] "Such scenes as the following, illustrating the beliefs of the time and the locality, would not seldom occur. A wayfarer in the country of the Getæ (Jats) (Afghanistan) knocks at the door of a Brahman family. A young man within answers: 'There is No One in this house.' The traveller was too well taught in Buddhism not to know the meaning of this philosophical nihilism, and at once answered, 'Who is No One?' The young man, when he heard this, felt that he was understood. A kindred spirit was outside. Hurriedly he opened the door, and invited the stranger to enter. The visitor was the patriarch of the time (seventeenth), with staff and rice bowl, travelling to teach and make new disciples."
—*Chinese Buddhism.* EDKINS.

Subhuti, if an enlightened disciple retains within his mind such arbitrary ideas of sentient life as an entity, a being, a living being, or a personality, he has not attained to supreme spiritual wisdom. And why? Because, Subhuti, there is no Law by means of which a disciple may be defined as one having obtained supreme spiritual wisdom."[1]

---

[1] Most writers on the Buddhist faith and religion have occasion to refer to the series of events which culminated in the Lord Buddha obtaining "supreme enlightenment." The founder of the Buddhist faith, dissatisfied with the practice of asceticism, and disappointed by his unfaithful disciples, walked meditatively towards the river Nairanjara, where Sujata, "the daughter of a neighbouring villager," provided him with his morning meal. Seating himself under a sacred Bo-Tree, immediately he became engaged in the severest of mental conflicts. The Buddhist authors describe their Master as sitting "sublime," "calm," and "serene" throughout the sustained assault of a "visible" and wicked tempter, assisted by legions of evil spirits. So unrelenting was the fierce encounter, that the forces of nature shook and were convulsed under the dreadful onslaught. As the day advanced, the spiritual elements in Buddha's nature gradually gained

The Lord Buddha addressed Subhuti, saying: "What think you? When the Lord Buddha was a disciple of Dipankara Buddha, was there bequeathed to him any Law whereby he attained to supreme spiritual wisdom?" Subhuti replied, saying: "No! Honoured of the Worlds! inasmuch as I am able to comprehend the meaning of the Lord Buddha's discourse, when the Lord Buddha was a disciple of Dipankara Buddha, there was no Law bequeathed to him whereby he attained to supreme spiritual wisdom."

the ascendency; and when he became "fully enlightened," there was revealed to him an antidote for human woe. The mind of the Lord Buddha thereafter assumed an aspect of perfect peace; "and in *the power over the human heart of inward culture, and of love to others,*" the great Teacher discovered a foundation of Truth, where, with assurance of faith, he could securely rest. As Milton regarded "Paradise" to be "regained" in the wilderness, and not on Calvary; in like manner the Buddhist poets indicate a belief that the experience of their Master under the Bo-Tree was the most eventful in his history. That is the reason they regard the Bo-Tree with a reverence resembling the Christian veneration of the Cross. (Compare Davids' *Buddhism.*)

The Lord Buddha endorsed these words, saying:[1] "Truly there is no Law by means of which the Lord Buddha obtained supreme spiritual wisdom. Subhuti, if there existed a Law by means of which the Lord Buddha obtained supreme spiritual wisdom, Dipankara Buddha would not have foretold at my initiation, 'In future ages[2] thou shalt become

---

[1] Buddha said: "Right! Right! Subhuti, there is in truth no fixed Law (by which) Tathagata attained this condition. Subhuti, if there had been such a Law, then Dipankara Buddha would not have said in delivering the prediction concerning me: 'you in after ages must attain to the state of Buddha, and your name shall be Sakyamuni,' so that because there is indeed no fixed Law for attaining the condition of 'the perfect heart,' on that account it was Dipankara Buddha delivered his prediction in such words."—*Kin-Kong-King*. BEAL.

[2] "To the pious Buddhist it is a constant source of joy and gratitude that 'the Buddha,' not only then, but in many former births, when emancipation from all the cares and troubles of life was already within his reach, should again and again, in mere love for man, have condescended to enter the world, and live amidst the sorrows inseparable from finite existence."—*Buddhism*. T. W. RHYS DAVIDS.

Sakyamuni Buddha.' But, in reality, there is no Law by means of which supreme spiritual wisdom can be obtained. Therefore, at my initiation, Dipankara Buddha foretold concerning me, 'In future ages, thou shalt become Sakyamuni Buddha.' And why? Because, in the word *Buddha*,[1] every Law

---

[1] "And why, O Subhuti, the name of Tathagata? It expresses 'true suchness.' And why Tathagata, O Subhuti? It expresses that 'he had no origin.' And why Tathagata, O Subhuti? It expresses 'the destruction of all qualities.' And why Tathagata, O Subhuti? It expresses 'one who has no origin whatever.' And why this? Because, O Subhuti, 'no origin is the highest goal.'"— *The Vagrakkhedika.* MAX MÜLLER.

The familiar word Buddha, seems to convey to devout Buddhist minds, a meaning consonant with the ethical idea of Love, as understood generally by the followers of Christ. Within it are potential spiritual elements, which, according to their judgment, perfectly fulfil the Law. The Chinese text, *Ju-Lai-che, chi-chu-fah-ru-i*, may bear the following interpretation, *Buddha is the One in whom all Laws become intelligible.* With this particular definition before us, and bearing in mind the general substance of the Mahayana faith, we may

is summarily and intelligibly comprehended."
"If a disciple affirmed that the Lord Buddha attained to supreme spiritual wisdom, it is necessary to state that there is no Law whereby this condition of mind can be realised. The supreme spiritual wisdom to which the Lord Buddha attained, cannot, in its essence, be defined as real or unreal. Thus, the Lord Buddha declared that the ordinarily accepted term, 'the Buddhic Law,' is synonymous with every moral and spiritual Law. Subhuti, what are ordinarily declared to be 'systems of Law,' are not in reality 'systems of Law,' they are merely termed 'systems of Law.'"

The Lord Buddha enquired of Subhuti, saying: "Can you imagine a man having a great physical body?" Subhuti replied, saying: "The Lord Buddha, discoursing upon the proportions of a physical body, did not main-

perhaps appreciate the sense in which the distinguished missionary, Dr Richard of Shanghai, ventured to render the Chinese term *Ju-Lai* (Buddha), in a translation of Asvaghocha's *The Awakening of Faith*, by the English synonym God. Few Christians would controvert the statement *that God is the One in whom all Laws become intelligible!*

tain for these any *real* greatness, therefore it is merely termed 'a great body.'"

The Lord Buddha, thereupon, addressed Subhuti, saying: "Thus it is with an enlightened disciple: if he were to expatiate after this manner, 'I must become oblivious to every idea of sentient life,'[1] he could not be described as fully enlightened. And why?

---

[1] "And if a Bodhisattva were to say: 'I shall deliver all beings,' he ought not to be called a Bodhisattva. And why? Is there anything, O Subhuti, that is called a Bodhisattva? Subhuti said: 'Not indeed!' Bhagavat said: 'Those who were spoken of as beings, beings indeed, O Subhuti, they were spoken of as no beings by the Tathagata, and, therefore, they are called beings. Therefore Tathagata says: "All beings are without self, all beings are without life, without manhood, without personality."'"—*The Vagrakkhedika.* MAX MÜLLER.

"Subhuti, so it is with the Bodhisatwa, if he should say: 'I ought to destroy all recollection of the countless kinds of creatures,' this Bodhisatwa would not be really one, but only a nominal one. . . . Hence Buddha says that all things ought to be without any individual distinction."— *Kin-Kong-King.* BEAL.

Because, there is no Law whereby a disciple can be approved as 'fully enlightened.'[1] Therefore, the Lord Buddha declared that within the realm of spiritual Law, there is neither an entity, a being, a living being, nor a personality."

The Lord Buddha addressed Subhuti, saying: "If an enlightened disciple were to speak in this wise, 'I shall create numerous Buddhist kingdoms,' he could not be designated 'fully enlightened.' And why? Because, the Lord Buddha, discoursing upon 'creating numerous Buddhist kingdoms,' did not affirm the idea of creating numerous 'material' Buddhist kingdoms, hence the 'creation of numerous Buddhist kingdoms' is merely a figure of speech. Subhuti, the Lord Buddha declared that a disciple may be regarded as 'truly enlightened,' whose mind is thoroughly imbued with the Law of non-individuality."[2]

---

[1] "The fountain of knowledge is the pure, bright, self-enlightening mind."—*Twan-Tsi-Sin-Yao* (*Tang* Dynasty). Compare Edkins' *Chinese Buddhism*.

[2] "A Bodhisattva, O Subhuti, who believes that all things are without self, he has faith, he is called a noble-minded Bodhisattva by

The Lord Buddha enquired of Subhuti, saying: "What think you? Does the Lord Buddha possess the physical eye?" Subhuti assented, saying: "Honoured of the Worlds! the Lord Buddha truly possesses the physical eye."

The Lord Buddha enquired of Subhuti, saying: "What think you? Does the Lord Buddha possess the divine or spiritual eye?" Subhuti assented, saying: "Honoured of the Worlds! the Lord Buddha truly possesses the divine or spiritual eye."

The Lord Buddha enquired of Subhuti, saying: "What think you? Does the Lord Buddha possess the eye of wisdom?" Subhuti assented, saying: "Honoured of the Worlds! the Lord Buddha truly possesses the eye of wisdom."

The Lord Buddha enquired of Subhuti, saying: "What think you? Does the Lord

the holy and fully enlightened Tathagata."—*The Vagrakkhedika.* MAX MÜLLER.

In the *Mo-Wei-Sutra*, the ordinary concepts of an entity, a being, a living being, or a personality, are referred to as *blots* or *stains* upon the mind.

Buddha possess the eye of truth?"[1] Subhuti assented, saying: "Honoured of the Worlds! the Lord Buddha truly possesses the eye of truth."

The Lord Buddha enquired of Subhuti, saying: "What think you? Does the Lord Buddha possess the Buddhic eye?" Subhuti assented, saying: "Honoured of the Worlds! the Lord Buddha truly possesses the Buddhic eye."[2]

---

[1] The Chinese *Fah-Yen*—literally, Eye of the Law.

"The second of the three great treasures is called *Dhamma*, or in Singhalese, *Dharmma*. This word has various meanings, but is here to be understood in the sense of Truth. It is not unfrequently translated 'the Law,' but this interpretation gives an idea contrary to the entire genius of Buddhism. The *Dharmma* is therefore emphatically the Truth."—*Eastern Monachism.* SPENCE HARDY.

[2] "Supernatural talents, which the founder of Buddhism, Sakyamuni, is believed to have acquired in the night before he became Buddha, and which every Arhat takes possession of by means of the fourth degree of *Dhyana* (abstract contemplation). Most Chinese texts reckon six such talents, while the Singhalese know only five. Sometimes,

The Lord Buddha enquired of Subhuti, saying: "What think you? Concerning the sands of the Ganges, did the Lord Buddha declare that these were grains of sand?" Subhuti assenting, said: "Honoured of the Worlds! the Lord Buddha declared that these were grains of sand."

The Lord Buddha enquired of Subhuti, saying: "What think you? If there were as many rivers Ganges as there are grains of sand in the Ganges, and if there were as many Buddhist worlds as the grains of sand in those innumerable rivers, would these Buddhist worlds be numerous?" Subhuti replied, saying: "Honoured of the Worlds! these Buddhist worlds would be very numerous."

The Lord Buddha, continuing, addressed

---

however, only five are mentioned."—*Handbook of Chinese Buddhism.* EITEL.

The physical eye has an ordinary local function. The divine or spiritual eye has a universal function. The eye of wisdom is affiliated with the Law, and attests its immutability. The eye of truth is exegetical and synthetical. The Buddhic eye is the instrument of salvation.—*Chinese Annotation.*

Subhuti, saying: "Within these innumerable worlds, every form of sentient life, with their various mental dispositions, are entirely known to the Lord Buddha.[1] And why? Because, what the Lord Buddha referred to as their 'various mental dispositions,' are not in reality

[1] "Bhagavat said, as many beings as there would be in all those worlds, I know the manifold trains of thought of them all. And why? Because, what was preached as the trains of thought, the trains of thought indeed, O Subhuti, that was preached by Tathagata as no train of thoughts, and therefore it is called the train of thoughts. And why? Because, O Subhuti, a past thought is not perceived, a future thought is not perceived, and the present thought is not perceived."—*The Vagrakkhedika.* MAX MÜLLER.

"Gautama himself was very early regarded as omniscient, and absolutely sinless. His perfect wisdom is declared by the ancient epithet of Samma-Sambuddha, 'the completely enlightened one,' found at the commencement of every Pali text; and at the present day in Ceylon, the usual way in which Gautama is styled is *Sarwajnan-Wahanse*, 'the venerable omniscient one.' From his perfect wisdom, according to Buddhist belief, his sinlessness would follow as a matter of course."—*Buddhism.* T. W. RHYS DAVIDS.

their 'various mental dispositions,' these are merely termed their 'various mental dispositions.' And why? Because, Subhuti, dispositions of mind, or modes of thought, whether relating to the past, the present, or the future, are alike unreal and illusory."

The Lord Buddha addressed Subhuti, saying: "What think you? If a disciple, having obtained all the treasures of this universe,[1] were to bestow these in the exercise of charity, would such a disciple consequently enjoy a considerable merit?" Subhuti assenting, said: "Honoured of the Worlds! such a disciple would consequently enjoy a very considerable merit."[2]

[1] The seven treasures—gold, silver, pearls, coral, cornelian, glass, and crystal.
[2] "Because, what was preached as a stock of merit, a stock of merit indeed, O Subhuti, that was preached as no-stock of merit by the Tathagata, and therefore it is called a stock of merit. If, O Subhuti, there existed a stock of merit, Tathagata would not have preached a stock of merit, a stock of

The Lord Buddha thereupon addressed Subhuti, saying: "If there were any real or permanent quality in merit, the Lord Buddha would not have spoken of such merit as 'considerable.' It is because there is neither a tangible nor material quality in merit, that the Lord Buddha referred to the merit of that disciple as 'considerable.'"

The Lord Buddha addressed Subhuti, saying: "What think you? Can the Lord Buddha be perceived by means of his perfect material body?"[1] Subhuti replied, saying:

merit indeed!"— *The Vagrakkhedika.*—MAX MÜLLER.

Within the meaning of the Buddhic Law, charity is purely a spiritual concept; and merit consequent upon fulfilling the Law of charity, must have a purely spiritual realisation. This is the sense in which the Lord Buddha referred to merit as "considerable." —*Chinese Annotation.*

[1] "The first of the Buddha's bodies is the *Dharma-Kaya* (body of the Law), supposed to be a kind of ethereal essence of a highly sublimated nature and co-extensive with space.

"Honoured of the Worlds! it is improbable that the Lord Buddha can be perceived by means of his perfect material body. And why? Because, what the Lord Buddha referred to as a 'perfect material body,' is not in reality a 'perfect material body,' it is merely termed a 'perfect material body.'"

The Lord Buddha addressed Subhuti, say-

This essence was believed to be eternal, and after the Buddha's death, was represented by the Law or doctrine (*Dharma*) he taught.

"The second body is the *Sambhoga-Kaya*, 'body of conscious bliss,' which is of a less ethereal and more material nature than the last. Its Brahmanical analogue appears to be the intermediate body (belonging to departed spirits) called *Bhoga - Deha*, which is of an ethereal character, though composed of sufficiently gross (Sthula) material particles to be capable of experiencing happiness or misery.

"The third body is the *Nirmana - Kaya*, 'body of visible shapes and transformations,' that is to say, those various concrete material forms in which every Buddha who exists as an invisible and eternal essence, is manifested on the earth or elsewhere for the propagation of the true doctrine."—*Buddhism.* Sir MONIER WILLIAMS.

ing: "What think you? Can the Lord Buddha be perceived by means of any physical phenomena?"[1] Subhuti replied, saying: "Honoured of the Worlds! it is improbable that the Lord Buddha can be perceived by means of any physical phenomena. And why? Because, what the Lord Buddha referred to as 'physical phenomena,' are not in reality 'physical phenomena,' these are merely termed 'physical phenomena.'"

---

[1] "What think you then, O Subhùti, is a Tathagata to be seen (known) by the shape of his visible body? Subhuti said, not indeed, a Tathagata is not to be seen (known) by the shape of his visible body. And why? Because, what was preached as the shape of the visible body, the shape of the visible body indeed, that was preached by Tathagata as no-shape of the visible body, and therefore it is called the shape of the visible body."— *The Vagrakkhedika.* MAX MÜLLER.

Herein is exemplification of the surpassing excellence of spiritual phenomena: although outwardly possessed of the thirty-two primal signs of a Buddha, there were also the essential evidences of those marvellous spiritual perfections which constitute the *real* Buddha. —*Chinese Annotation.*

The Lord Buddha addressed Subhuti, saying: "Do not affirm that the Lord Buddha thinks thus within himself, 'I ought to promulgate a system of Law or doctrine.' Have no such irrelevant thought! And why? Because, if a disciple affirmed that the Lord Buddha promulgated a system of Law or doctrine, he would defame the Lord Buddha, being manifestly unable to understand the purport of my instruction. Subhuti, regarding the promulgation of a 'system of Law or doctrine,' there is in reality no 'system of Law or doctrine' to promulgate, it is merely termed a 'system of Law or doctrine.'"[1]

---

[1] "Bhagavat said: What do you think, O Subhuti, does Tathagata think in this wise: the Law has been taught by me? Subhuti said: Not indeed, O Bhagavat, does the Tathagata think in this wise: the Law has been taught by me. Bhagavat said: If a man should say that the Law has been taught by the Tathagata, he would say what is not true; he would slander me with untruth which he has learned. And why? Because, O Subhuti, it is said the teaching of the Law, the teaching of the Law indeed, O Subhuti, there is

Upon that occasion, the virtuous and venerable Subhuti enquired of the Lord Buddha, saying: "Honoured of the Worlds! in ages to come, will sentient beings destined to hear this Law,[1] engender within their minds the essential elements of faith?" The Lord Buddha replied, saying: "Subhuti, it cannot be asserted that these are sentient beings, or that these are not sentient beings. And why? Because, Subhuti, regarding 'sentient beings,' the Lord Buddha declared that in reality these are not 'sentient

nothing that can be perceived by the name of the teaching of the Law."—*The Vagrakkhedika.* MAX MÜLLER.

Eminent wisdom possesses the natural beauty of a pellucid stream, flowing swiftly between rugged mountain crags; but a mind at rest from 'systems of Law or doctrine,' is reminiscent of the loveliness of a waterfall, frozen into shining icicles, and resplendent in the light of the moon. — *Chinese Annotation.*

[1] "He is the best of all guides of men, no other being is like unto him; he is like a jewel, of imperishable glory, who hears this Law with a pure heart."—*The Buddha-Karita.* E. B. COWELL.

beings,' they are merely termed 'sentient beings.'"[1]

Subhuti enquired of the Lord Buddha, saying: "Honoured of the Worlds! did the Lord Buddha, in attaining to supreme spiritual wisdom, obtain nothing of a real or tangible nature?" The Lord Buddha replied, saying: "In attaining to supreme spiritual wisdom, not a vestige of Law or doctrine was obtained,[2] and therefore it is termed 'supreme spiritual wisdom.'"

---

[1] "Bhagavat said: These, O Subhuti, are neither beings nor no-beings. And why? Because, O Subhuti, those who were preached as beings, beings indeed, they were preached as no-beings by the Tathagata, and therefore they are called beings."—*The Vagrakkhedika.* MAX MÜLLER.

Although these are ordinarily referred to as sentient beings, there are spiritual elements in their real natures, which place them in a category only imperfectly described by the term "sentient beings"; but possessing also evident material qualities, it might be an error to assert that these are not "sentient beings"; hence the declaration of the Lord Buddha, "they are merely termed sentient beings."—*Chinese Annotation.*

[2] "To affirm the existence of anything real or

The Lord Buddha addressed Subhuti, saying: "This Law is coherent and indivisible,[1] it is neither 'above' nor 'below,'[2] therefore tangible in the nature of the Law, would be tantamount to being firmly bound by the Law; but to affirm that 'not even the vestige of Law or doctrine was obtained,' is the equivalent of being absolutely free from the Law."—*Yen-Ping* (a Chinese monk).

"Buddha said: 'True, true, Subhuti! I, as possessed of this heart, have come into the condition above described. This term the unsurpassed, just, and enlightened heart, is but a mere name.'"—*Kin-Kong-King*. BEAL.

[1] The Abbé Dubois in his valuable book, *Hindu Manners, Customs, and Ceremonies*, carefully observes that amongst the attributes which the Jains ascribe to the Supreme Being, the first is that He is "one" and "indivisible"; and this observation of the learned Abbé becomes quite illuminating, when we remember the intimate relationship which has existed between the Jains and the Law of Buddha.

[2] "Within it first arose desire, the primal germ of mind,
Which nothing with existence links, as sages searching find.
The cord, transversely stretched, that spanned this universal frame,
Was it beneath? was it above? can any sage proclaim?"

it is termed 'supreme spiritual wisdom.' It excludes such arbitrary ideas as an entity, a being, a living being, or a personality; but includes every Law pertaining to the cultivation of goodness.[1] Subhuti, what were referred to as 'Laws pertaining to goodness,' these the Lord Buddha declared are not in reality 'Laws

"Progress of the Vedic religion towards abstract conceptions of the Deity." J. MUIR (*Journal of the Royal Asiatic Society*).

[1] "Free from self, free from life, free from personality, that highest perfect knowledge is always the same, and thus known with all good things. And why? Because, what was preached as good things, good things, indeed, O Subhuti, they were preached by the Tathagata as no-things, and therefore are they called good things." — *The Vagrakkhedika.* MAX MÜLLER.

"This condition which is named the unsurpassed, just, and enlightened (heart), consists in nothing more than the exclusion of all individual distinctions. A man who practices all the rules of virtuous conduct will forthwith attain this condition. But, Subhuti, when we speak of rules of virtuous conduct, Tathagata declares that these rules are after all no real and lasting rules; the term is but a mere name."—*Kin-Kong-King.* BEAL.

pertaining to goodness,' they are merely termed 'Laws pertaining to goodness.'"[1]

The Lord Buddha addressed Subhuti, saying: "If within this universe of universes, the seven treasures[2] were heaped together, forming as many great elevations as there are Sumerus, prince of mountains, and these treasures bestowed entirely in the exercise of charity; and if a disciple were to select a stanza of this Scripture, rigorously observe it, and diligently explain it to others, the merit[3] thus obtained would so far exceed the

---

[1] The six *Paramita*—charity, morality, endurance, energy, contemplation, wisdom, comprehended under the term "Laws pertaining to goodness," merely constitute an open door by means of which disciples are ushered into the presence of truth.—*Chinese Annotation*.

[2] Gold, silver, pearls, coral, cornelian, glass, and crystal.

[3] "And whosoever in days when the good Law is abolished, abandons love for his own body and life, and proclaims day and night these good words—pre-eminent is his merit from this.

"He obtains a glorious and endless splendour

THE DIAMOND SUTRA 91

former excellence, that it cannot be stated in terms of proportion, nor comprehended by any analogy."[1]

The Lord Buddha addressed Subhuti, saying: "What think you? You disciples, do not affirm that the Lord Buddha reflects thus within himself, 'I bring salvation to every living being.' Subhuti, entertain no such delusive thought! And why? Because, in reality there are no living beings to whom the

who teaches even one word thereof; he will not miss one consonant nor the meaning who gives this Sutra to others.

"Therefore let those who are endowed with lofty ambitions, always hear this Law which causes transcendent merit; let them hear it and gladly welcome it and lay it up in their minds and continually worship the three jewels (the Buddha, the Law, and the assembly of monks) with faith."—*Buddha-Karita*. E. B. COWELL.

[1] "I declare that his happiness and consequent merit would be incomparably greater than that of the other, so much so, that no number could express the excess of one over the other."—*Kin-Kong-King*. BEAL.

Lord Buddha can bring salvation.[1] If there were living beings to whom the Lord Buddha

[1] As the primordial human mind is void and quiescent, so also is the wisdom of this Sutra full and overflowing. Therefore, hearing the text of this Sutra expounded, and meditating upon its truth, there are formed spontaneously within the minds of those living beings, all the essential elements of salvation. As these mature and develop into a Law of spiritual liberty, the Lord Buddha obviously relinquishes every duty consonant with the idea of a delegated Saviour.—*Chinese Annotation.*

"What do you think then, O Subhuti, does a Tathagata think in this wise: beings have been delivered by me? You should not think so. And why? Because, there is no being that has been delivered by the Tathagata. And if there were a being, O Subhuti, that had been delivered by the Tathagata, then Tathagata would believe in a self, a being, a living being, and a person. And what is called a belief in self, O Subhuti, that is preached as a no-belief by the Tathagata. And this is learned by children and ignorant persons, and they who were preached as children and ignorant persons, O Subhuti, were preached as no-persons by the Tathagata, and therefore they are called children and ignorant persons."
—*The Vagrakkhedika.* MAX MÜLLER.

could bring salvation, the Lord Buddha would necessarily assume the reality of such arbitrary concepts as an entity, a being, a living being, and a personality. Subhuti, what the Lord Buddha adverted to as an entity, is not in reality an entity; it is only understood to be an entity, and believed in as such, by the common, uneducated people. Subhuti, what are ordinarily referred to as the 'common, uneducated people,' these the Lord Buddha declared to be not merely 'common, uneducated people.'"[1]

The Lord Buddha addressed Subhuti, saying: "Can the Lord Buddha be perceived

[1] "Difference there is in beings endowed with bodies, but amongst men this is not the case, the difference amongst men is nominal only."—*Dhammapada.* MAX MÜLLER.

"Wordly profit is fleeting and perishable, religious (holy) profit is eternal and inexhaustible; a man though a king is full of trouble, a common man who is holy, has everlasting rest." — *Fo-Sho-Hing-Tsan-King.* BEAL.

94 THE DIAMOND SUTRA

by means of his thirty-two bodily distinctions?"[1] Subhuti replied, saying: "Even so,[2] the Lord Buddha can be perceived by means of his thirty-two bodily distinctions."

The Lord Buddha, continuing, said unto Subhuti: "If by means of his thirty-two bodily distinctions it were possible to perceive the Lord Buddha, then the Lord Buddha would merely resemble one of the great wheel-turning kings."[3]

---

[1] "This probably refers to the auspicious signs discovered in Sakyamuni at his birth, which left it open whether he would become a king or a Buddha."—*The Vagrakkhedika.* MAX MÜLLER.

[2] Subhuti failed to apprehend the idea as expressed by the Lord Buddha, and inadvertently replied, saying: "Even so, Even so."—*Chinese Annotation.*

[3] "The protends troubled, till his dream-readers
    Augured a prince of earthly dominance,
    A Chakravartin, such as rise to rule
    Once in a thousand years."

—*The Light of Asia.* Sir EDWIN ARNOLD.

"A king who rules the world, and causes the wheel of doctrine everywhere to revolve. The great Asoka (King of Central India, who reigned near Patna, about 150-200 years after the demise of Buddha) was a 'wheel

Subhuti thereupon addressed the Lord Buddha, saying: "Honoured of the Worlds! According as I am able to interpret the Lord Buddha's instruction, it is improbable that the Lord Buddha may be perceived by means of his thirty-two bodily distinctions."

Thereafter, the "Honoured of the Worlds" delivered this sublime Gatha:

"*I am not to be perceived by means of any visible form,*
Nor sought after by means of any audible sound;
Whosoever walks in the way of iniquity,
Cannot perceive the blessedness of the Lord Buddha."[1]

king.' The word is Chakravarti in Sanscrit, from Chakra 'wheel,' the symbol of activity, whether of Buddha in preaching, or of kings like Asoka in ruling."—*Chinese Buddhism.* EDKINS.

"Those of the Bikkhus who carry in their hearts the words of excellent knowledge that is immeasurable, who are free from bonds, whose fame and power and glory no man can weigh, who (in imitation of their master) keep the royal chariot wheel of the kingdom of righteousness rolling on, who have reached perfection in knowledge."—*Questions of King Milinda.* T. W. RHYS DAVIDS.

[1] The following Gatha, translated by Max Müller, and concluding the twenty-sixth section

The Lord Buddha said unto Subhuti: "If you think thus within yourself 'The Lord Buddha did not, by means of his perfect bodily distinctions, obtain supreme spiritual wisdom,' Subhuti, have no such deceptive thought! Or if you think thus within yourself, 'In obtaining supreme spiritual wisdom, the Lord Buddha declared the abrogation of every Law,' Subhuti, have no such delusive thought! And why? Because, those disciples who obtain supreme spiritual wisdom, neither affirm the abrogation of any Law, nor the destruction of any distinctive quality of phenomena."[1]

---

of *The Vagrakkhedika*, is not incorporated in the Chinese text.

"A Buddha is to be seen (known) from the Law;
For the Lords (Buddha) have the Law-Body;
And the nature of the Law cannot be understood,
Nor can it be made to be understood."

[1] "What do you think then, O Subhuti, has the highest perfect knowledge been known by the Tathagata by the possession of signs? You should not think so, O Subhuti. And why? Because, the highest perfect knowledge will not be known by the Tathagata through the possession of signs. Nor should anybody,

The Lord Buddha addressed Subhuti, saying: "If an enlightened disciple, in the exercise of

O Subhuti, say to you that the destruction or annihilation of anything is proclaimed by those who have entered on the path of the Bodhisattvas."— *The Vagrakkhedika.* MAX MÜLLER.

"Subhuti, if you should think thus, 'Tathagata, by means of his personal distinctions has attained to the unsurpassable condition,' you would be wrong. . . . But, Subhuti, do not come to such an opinion as this, viz., 'that what is called the unsurpassed, just, and enlightened heart is nothing more than the mere neglect and destruction of all rules and conditions.' Think not so, for why? the exhibition of this perfect and unsurpassed heart is not the consequence of having disregarded and destroyed all rules, in the active discharge of duty."—*Kin-Kong-King.* BEAL.

Concerning the phenomena of Law, if these were abrogated and entirely discarded, where would the mind receive its guiding light, or the human spirit its power of discernment? To attempt a process of reasoning apart from such necessary postulates as the distinctive qualities of Law and phenomena, would prove to be as futile as an effort to cross a river without a raft, and would inevitably end in oblivion.—*Chinese Annotation.*

charity, bestowed as considerable an amount of the seven treasures as might fill worlds numerous as the sands of the Ganges; and if a disciple, realising that within the meaning and purport of the Law, there is no abstract individual existence,[1] perfects himself in the virtue of endurance, this latter disciple will have a cumulative merit, relatively greater than the other. And why? Because, enlightened disciples are entirely unaffected by considerations of 'reward or merit.'"

Subhuti thereupon enquired of the Lord Buddha, saying: "Honoured of the Worlds! in what respect are enlightened disciples unaffected by considerations of 'reward or merit'?" The Lord Buddha replied, saying:

---

[1] "And if a Bodhisattva acquired endurance in selfless and uncreated things, then he would enjoy a larger stock of merit, immeasurable and innumerable."—*The Vagrakkhedika.* MAX MÜLLER.
 "Nothing in this world is single,
   All things by a law divine
   In one another's being mingle."—SHELLEY.

"Enlightened disciples do not aspire, in a spirit of covetousness, to rewards commensurate with their merit; therefore, I declare that they are entirely unaffected by considerations of 'reward or merit.'"[1]

The Lord Buddha addressed Subhuti, saying: "If a disciple asserts that the Lord Buddha comes or goes, sits or reclines, obviously he has not understood the meaning of my discourse. And why? Because, the

[1] "Subhuti asked Buddha: World-honoured One! what is this you say, that Bodhisatwas cannot be said to appreciate reward? 'Subhuti, the reward which a Bodhisatwa enjoys ought to be connected with no covetous desire; this is what I mean by non-appreciation of reward.'" —*Kin-Kong-King*. BEAL.

This passage, concluding the twenty-eighth section of *The Diamond Sutra*, not being incorporated in the translation of *The Vagrakkhedika* by Max Müller, may be suggestive of a noteworthy interpolation in the Chinese text, or is it a probable lacuna in the Sanscrit MSS.?

idea 'Buddha' implies neither coming from anywhere, nor going to anywhere, and hence the synonym 'Buddha!'"[1]

---

[1] "And why? Because the word Tathagata means one who does not go to anywhere, and does not come from anywhere, and therefore he is called the Tathagata (truly come), holy and fully enlightened."—*The Vagrakkhedika.* MAX MÜLLER.

"That which is Tathagata has no where whence to come, and no where whither he can go, and is therefore named Tathagata." —*Kin-Kong-King.* BEAL.

In the heavens above, we cannot discern a place whence he came, nor whither he may return. In his holy, immaculate, and marvellously endowed body, were manifested plenary spiritual powers.—*Hua-Yen-Sutra.*

Like drifting clouds, like the waning moon, like ships that sail the ocean, like shores that are washed away—these are symbolic of endless change. But the blessed Buddha, in his essential, absolute nature, is changeless and everlasting.—*Yuen-Chioh-Sutra.*

"If the pool be of pure water, the shining moon is reflected upon its limpid surface; and yet we cannot affirm that the moon really came from anywhere, or that it is actually in the pool. If the pool be disturbed and the dense mud raised, immediately the bright reflection

The Lord Buddha addressed Subhuti, saying: "If a good disciple, whether man or woman, were to take infinite worlds and 'reduce' them to minute particles of dust; what think you, would the aggregate of all those particles of dust be great?" Subhuti replied, saying: "Honoured of the Worlds! the aggregate of all those particles of dust would be exceedingly great. And why? Because, if all those were in reality 'minute particles of dust,' the Lord Buddha would not have declared them to be 'minute particles of dust.' And why? Because, the Lord Buddha, discoursing upon 'minute particles of dust,' declared that in reality those

becomes obscured; and yet we dare not affirm that the moon has really gone to anywhere, or that it has actually departed from the pool. It is entirely a question of the purity or impurity of the water, and has no reasonable affinity with theories concerning the existence or non-existence of the moon. So, also, with the true concept of Buddha; only those whose minds are immaculate in their pristine purity, can ever realise his transcendent blessedness." — *Chang-Shui* (a Chinese monk).

are not 'minute particles of dust,' they are merely termed 'minute particles of dust.'"[1]

Subhuti continuing, addressed the Lord Buddha, saying: "Honoured of the Worlds! what the Lord Buddha discoursed upon as 'infinite worlds,' these are not in reality

[1] These minute particles of dust, like the great worlds which are composed of them, are deceptive forms of natural phenomena, equally unreal and evanescent. The minute particles which we observe floating in space, are carried hither and thither by atmospheric currents, and eventually pass into regions beyond our cognisance. So, also, with the immense worlds revolving in space; their ever-recurring phenomena of light and darkness, heat and cold, changing seasons, transient scenes of mountain and valley, river and plain. These things indicate that all are ephemeral, and entirely subject to irrevocable laws of change and decay.—*Chinese Annotation.*

"Because, what was preached as a mass of many atoms by the Tathagata, that was preached as no-mass of atoms by the Tathagata, and therefore it is called 'a mass of many atoms.'"—*The Vagrakkhedika.* MAX MÜLLER.

"What then, if Buddha speaks of all these particles, then they are not really what they are called, it is but a mere name, World-Honoured One!"—*Kin-Kong-King.* BEAL.

'infinite worlds,' they are merely termed 'infinite worlds.' And why? Because, if these were in reality 'infinite worlds,' there would of necessity be unity and eternity of matter. But the Lord Buddha, discoursing upon the 'unity and eternity of matter,' declared that there is neither 'unity' nor 'eternity of matter,' therefore it is merely termed 'unity and eternity of matter.'"

The Lord Buddha thereupon declared unto Subhuti, "Belief in the unity or eternity of matter is incomprehensible;[1] and only common,

---

[1] "Bhagavat said, and a belief in matter itself, O Subhuti, is inestimable and inexpressible; it is neither a thing nor a no-thing, and this is known by children and ignorant persons."— *The Vagrakkhedika.* MAX MÜLLER.

"Annihilation of matter is inconceivable, but annihilation of all its forms and qualities is conceivable." *The World as Idea and Will.* SCHOPENHAUER.

If the worlds were real and permanent, they would always retain their original forms and primordial natures, and be subject neither to the influence of time nor the Law of change.—*Chinese Annotation.*

"Subhuti, this characteristic of the one 'harmonious principle,' is a thing which cannot worldly-minded people, for purely materialistic reasons, covet this hypothesis."

The Lord Buddha addressed Suhhuti, saying: "If a disciple affirmed that the Lord

be spoken of in words; it is only the vain philosophy of the world, which has grasped the idea of explaining this."—*Kin-Kong-King*. BEAL.

This noteworthy statement seems to militate against some opinions expressed in Europe regarding the Buddhist theory of "matter." According to our Chinese text, it does not appear that Sakyamuni Buddha categorically denied the "presence" or "existence" of matter in the universe, but endeavoured rather to indicate the diversified and evanescent nature of its "forms" and "qualities." Many devout Buddhists regard even the smallest particle of dust as containing a mysterious and elusive element—probably what we are disposed to term "a spiritual element," or "principle of life"—and these are not unreasonably regarded as being altogether inscrutable, and therefore "incomprehensible."

Buddha enunciated a belief[1] that the mind can comprehend the idea of an entity, a being, a living being, or a personality; what think you, Subhuti, would that disciple be interpret-

[1] "Because, O Subhuti, if a man were to say that belief in self, belief in a being, belief in life, belief in personality, had been preached by the Tathagata, would he be speaking truly? Subhuti said, not indeed, Bhagavat, he would not be speaking truly. And why? Because, what was preached by the Tathagata as a belief in self, that was preached as no-belief, therefore it is called belief in self."—*The Vagrakkhedika.* MAX MÜLLER.

In these words are exemplified another profound aspect of Buddhist doctrine. Apart from interesting questions concerning the existence of an entity, a being, a living being, or a personality, another problem seems to arise regarding our ability to entirely perceive or "comprehend" those admitted abstract ideas. If we interpret aright the Buddhist doctrine, there are variously compounded within those abstract ideas, so many elusive spiritual elements, that the human mind is incapable of resolving them by any process of reasoning. In short—an entity, a being, a living being, or a personality, represents to the Buddhist mind, much more than it attempts to express in terms of philosophy.

ing aright the meaning of my discourse?" Subhuti replied, saying: "Honoured of the Worlds! that disciple would not be interpreting aright the meaning of the Lord Buddha's discourse. And why? Because, Honoured of the Worlds! discoursing upon comprehending such ideas as an entity, a being, a living being, and a personality, it was declared that these are entirely unreal and illusive, and therefore they are merely termed an entity, a being, a living being, and a personality."

The Lord Buddha thereafter addressed Subhuti, saying:[1] "Those who aspire to the

---

[1] "Thus then, O Subhuti, are all things to be perceived, to be looked upon, and to be believed by one who has entered upon the path of the Bodhisattvas. And in this wise are they to be perceived, to be looked upon, and to be believed, neither in the idea of a thing, nor in the idea of a no-thing? And why? Because by saying: the idea of a thing, the idea of a thing indeed, it has been preached by the Tathagata as the no-idea of a thing."—*The Vagrakkhedika.* MAX MÜLLER.

"Subhuti, the persons who aspire to the perfectly enlightened heart, ought to know accordingly that this is true with respect to attainment of supreme spiritual wisdom ought thus to know, believe in, and interpret phenomena. They ought to eliminate from their minds every tangible evidence of every visible object. Subhuti, concerning 'visible objects,' the Lord Buddha declared that these are not really 'visible objects,' they are merely termed 'visible objects.'"

The Lord Buddha addressed Subhuti, saying: "If a disciple, having immeasurable spheres filled with the seven treasures,[1] bestowed these in the exercise of charity; and if a disciple, whether man or woman, having aspired to supreme spiritual wisdom, selected from this Scripture a stanza comprising four lines, then rigorously observed

all things, and thus prevent the exhibition of any characteristics on any point whatever. Subhuti, these very characteristics of which we speak are after all no characteristics, but a mere name."—*Kin-Kong-King*. BEAL.

[1] Gold, silver, pearls, coral, cornelian, glass, and crystal.

it, studied it, and diligently explained it to others; the cumulative merit of such a disciple would be relatively greater than the other."

"In what attitude of mind should it be diligently explained to others?[1] Not assuming the permanency or the reality of earthly phenomena, but in the conscious blessedness of a mind at perfect rest.[2] And why? Because,

---

[1] "The wise man, the preacher, who wishes to expound this Sutra, must absolutely renounce falsehood, pride, calumny, and envy. . . . He is always sincere, mild, forbearing; . . . he must feel affection for all beings who are striving for enlightenment . . . they are greatly perverted in their minds, those beings who do not hear, nor perceive . . . the mystery of the Tathagata. Nevertheless will I, who have attained this supreme, perfect knowledge, powerfully bend to it the mind of every one (Burnouf, *par la force de mes facultés surnaturelles*), whatever may be the position he occupies, and bring about that he accepts, understands, and arrives at full ripeness." — *Saddharma - Pundarika.* H. KERN.

[2] "By contemplation are obtained those conditions through which is eventually gained that supreme calm, undecaying, immortal state,

the phenomena of life may be likened unto a dream, a phantasm, a bubble,[1] a shadow,

which is so hard to be reached."—*Buddha-Karita.* E. B. COWELL.

"And in what way can the disciple 'proclaim them generally?' Simply by relying on no conditions or distinctions whatever; thus he will act without agitation or excitement. Wherefore the conclusion is this—that all things which admit of definition are as a dream, a phantom, a bubble, a shadow, as the dew and lightning flash. They ought to be regarded thus."—*Kin-Kong-King.* BEAL.

"And how should he explain it? As in the sky: stars, darkness, a lamp, a phantom, dew, a bubble, a dream, a flash of lightning, and a cloud—thus should we look upon the world (all that was made).—*The Vagrakkhedika.* MAX MÜLLER.

[1] "*Fa-Hien* stayed at the dragon Vihara till after the summer retreat, and then, travelling to the south-east for seven Yojanas, he arrived at the city of Kanyakubja, lying along the Ganges. . . . At a distance from the city of six or seven *Le*, on the west, on the northern bank of the Ganges, is a place where Buddha preached the Law to his disciples. It has been handed down that his subjects of discourse were such as 'The bitterness and vanity (of life), as impermanent and uncertain,' and that 'The body is as a "bubble" or foam on the water.'"—*Travels of Fa-Hien.* LEGGE.

the glistening dew, or lightning flash, and thus they ought to be contemplated."

When the Lord Buddha concluded his enunciation of this Scripture,[1] the venerable Subhuti, the monks,[2] nuns, lay-brethren and sisters, all mortals, and the whole realm of spiritual beings, rejoiced exceedingly, and consecrated to its practice, they received it and departed.

---

[1] "Thus spake the Bhagavat enraptured; the elder Subhuti, and the friars, nuns, the faithful lay men and women, and the Bodhisattvas also, and the whole world of gods, men, evil spirits and fairies, praised the preaching of the Bhagavat."—*The Vagrakkhedika.* MAX MÜLLER.

[2] "The vow of 'obedience' was never taken by the Buddhist monks and nuns, and in this it may be noticed a fundamental difference between them and monastic orders in the West: mental culture, not mental death, was the aim set before the Buddhist ascetic by the founder of his faith."—*Buddhism.* T. W. RHYS DAVIDS.

"As when men, travelling, feel a glorious perfume sweet
  Pervading all the country side, and gladdening them, infer at once,
'Surely 'tis giant forest trees are flowering now!'
  So, conscious of this perfume sweet of righteousness
  That now pervades the earth and heavens, they may infer:
'A Buddha, infinitely great, must once have lived!'"

INDEX

ALEXANDRIA, 20
Alms-bowl, 3, 5
Almsgiving, 2
Anagami, 31, 32
Ananda, 11, 12
Anepidu, 51
Anniversaries, 37
Anta-Kalpas, 42
Anuradhapura, 51
Anurogrammum, 51
Apatti, 28
Aranyaka, 35, 36, 37
Arhat, 31, 32, 33, 34, 35, 55, 78
Ari-Hat, 32
Arjuna, 57
Arnold (Sir Edwin), 11, 18, 21, 29, 40, 42, 48, 50, 55, 94
Arya, 31, 32
Aryagiti, 26
Arya-Marga, 32
Ascetic, 21
Asiatic, 89
Asoka, 94, 95
Asurus, 44
Asvaghocha, 9, 74
Atman, 51
Atoms, 48
Attavada, 12
αὐτοδίδακτος, 38
Awakening of Faith, 9, 74

Bacche (The), 20
Bana, 35, 45, 51
Beal, 7, 10, 15, 24, 26, 28, 36, 39, 43, 45, 49, 50, etc.

Benares, 1
Benefactions, 3
Bhagavad-Gita, 8, 23, 34, 58, 68
Bhagavat, 23, 26, 38, 47, 54, 80, 85, 87, 103, 105, 110
Bhoga-Deha, 83
Bikkhus, 95
Bikshu, 7
Bikshuni, 7
Bodhi, 6, 35, 62, 63
Bodhisattva, 6, 38, 39, 58, 59, 69, 75, 76, 97, 98, 99, 106, 110
Bo-Tree, 70, 71
Brahman, 69
Brahmanas, 1
Brahmanical, 83
Brahmanism, 17
Buddha, 1, 3, 4, 5, 8, 9, 18, etc.
Buddha-Karita, 86, 91, 109
Buddhaphalam, 32
Buddhas, 7, 11, 25, 28
Buddhaship, 6, 15, 32
Buddhic, 27
Buddhism, 13, 14, 16, 19, 41, 49, 63, 72, 80, 83, 110
Burnouf, 108

Calingapatah, 56
Calvary, 71
Ceylon, 80
Ceylon Friend, 61
Chakra, 95
Chakravartin, 94, 95

Chang-Ming, 20
Chang-Shui, 101
Chiliocosms, 43, 49
China, 5, 18
Chinese Buddhism, 2, 7, 9, 37, 39, 40, 69
Chioh-Hsien, 11
Christ, 8, 23, 40, 63, 73
Christians, 74
Chuan-Fah-Luen, 14
Chuang-Yen, 39
Circars, 56
Coral, 25, 43, 64, 81, 108
Cornelian, 25, 43, 64, 81, 108
Cowell, E. B., 86, 91, 109
Creed, 47
Cross, 71
Crystal, 25, 43, 64, 81, 108

Danataka Aranyaka, 35
Davids, T. W. Rhys, 13, 29, 31, 80, 95, 110
Davis, Sir John Francis, 19
Dewa-Loka, 30
Devas, 31
Dhamma, 27, 34, 44, 52
Dhammapada, 34, 44, 52, 63, 93
Dhammo, 78
Dharma, 30, 35, 83
Dharma Aranyaka, 35
Dharma-Kaya, 17, 82
Dharmasala, 65
Dharmma, 27
Diamond Sutra, The, 37, 47
Dipankara Buddha, 37, 38, 67, 71, 72, 73
Djatakas, 2
Dubois (the Abbé), 88

Eastern Monachism, 4, 5, 16, 21, 27, 30, 35, 36, 38, 46, 51, 53, 61, 78
Edkins, 2, 7, 9, 39, 40, 69
Egypt, 20

Eitel, 1, 2, 6, 11, 13, 26, 28, 31, 32, 35, 37, 49, 56, 57, 58, 79
Elburz, 40
Eleusis, 65
Enlightenment of Ananda, 12
Euripides, 20
Europe, 20, 104

Fa-Hien, 2, 65, 109
Fah, 14, 60
Fah-Ai, 14
Fah-Lien, 14
Fah-Luen, 14
Fah-Men, 14
Fah-Ming, 14
Fah-Pao, 14
Fah-Shen, 16
Fah-Wang, 14
Fah-Yen, 78
Fairies, 110
Faith, 3, 27
Fausböll, 23, 27
Fei-Fuh-Fah, 28
Fo-Sho-Hing-Tsan-King, 93
Fox, 68
Fuh-Ko, 32
Fuh-Tu, 39

Gandhara, 5
Ganges, 2, 42, 51, 61, 79, 98, 109
Gatha, 26, 95
Gautama, 63, 80
German, 20
Getæ, 69
Girdle, 3
Glass, 25, 43, 64, 81, 108
God, 21, 74
Gods, 110
Gogerly, Rev. D. J., 61
Gold, 25, 43, 64, 81, 108
Gondophares, 9
Gotama, 52
Greek, 20
Gunga, 42

INDEX

Hardy, Spence, 4, 16, 21, 27, 30, 35, 36, 38, 46, 51, 53, 61, 78
Hastigiri, 48
Hero, 50
Hinayana, 64
Hindoo, 64
Hindu Manners, Customs, and Ceremonies, 88
Hinduism, 66
Hiuen-Tsang, 2, 50, 53, 65
Ho-Ru-To-Lo-San-Mao-San-Pu-Ti, 7
Ho-Tan-Ju-Lai, 63
Hua-Yen-Sutra, 100
Hunter, Sir William, 55
Huxley, 10

Icicles, 86
Idea and Will, The World as, 48, 103
Immortality, 44
Immortals, 2
India, 7, 20
Indian Empire, The, 55
Indo-Scythic, 9
I-Wu-Wei-Fah, 25

Jains, 88
Jayendra, 53
Jesus, 18
Jeta, 2, 4
Jewels, 91

Kalinga, 56
Kaliradja, 56
Kalpa, 45
Kanyakubja, 109
Kashaya, 50
Kasina, 36
Kasmir, 65
Kern, H., 39, 58, 108
Khaloupas' Waddhaktinka, 4
Kin-Kong-King, 7, 10, 15, 24, 26, 28, 36, 39, 45, 49, 50, etc.

Kingdoms, 38, 40, 76
Kos'ala, 56
Kshanti, 58
Kshantivadin, 58
Kwa-Yuh, 33

Lao-Tsz, 28
Lay Sermons, 10
Le, 109
Legge, 65, 109
Light of Asia (The), 11, 18, 21, 29, 34, 40, 42, 48, 50, 55, 94, etc.
Lotus of the Good Law, 64
Love, 73

Ma-Ming, 9
Madhyades'a, 5
Mahasattvas, 7
Mahayana, 62
Mantras, 1
Matanga, 35
Materialist, 48
Maya, 50, 58
Meitreya (Buddha), 4
Memoirs sur les Contrées Occidentales, 2
Mencius, 33
Mendicant, 4
Metamorphosis, 9
Mieh-Tu, 10
Milinda, 4, 29, 31, 33, 36, 95
Milton, 71
Mo-Ho-Sa, 7
Mo-Wei-Sutra, 77
Muir (J.), 89
Müller (Max), 1, 25, 26, 30, 34, 39, 42, 44, 46, 52, 54, etc.
Murray (Gilbert), 20
Myak, 7

Nairanjara, 70
Narakas, 46
Needle, 3
Nibbana, 23
Nihilism, 69

INDEX

Nimitta, 36
Nirmanakaya, 17, 83
Nirvana, 1, 7, 8, 10, 11, 17, 18, 23, 27, 28, 30, 31, 32, 44, 46, 55, 62, 63, 69
Non-individuality, 76
Nuttara, 7

Œdipus Coloneus, 65
O-siu-lo, 44

Padumas, 48
Pali, 80
Paramita, 13, 55, 56, 90
Patna, 94
Path, 18
Paul (The Apostle), 8, 23
Pearls, 25, 43, 64, 81, 108
Persia, 5
Pilgrims, 2
Po-Ro-Po-Lo-Mi, 8
Prajna-Paramita, 9
Prakrita, 57
Prasenajit, 2
Priests, 4
Ptolemy, 51
Puh-Seng, 32
Pundarikas, 48
Pu-sa, 6

Questions of King Milinda, 4, 29, 31, 33, 36, 95

Raft, 23
Rahat, 20
Rahatship, 35
Ran-Teng-Fuh, 37
Razor, 3
Regents, 40
Reincarnation, 30, 31
Relation des Royaumes Buddhiques, 5
Remusat, 5
Ren, 44
Richard (Dr), 74
Righteousness, 33

Rishi, 58
Robe, 3, 4

Saddharma-Pundarika, 39, 54, 58, 108
Sagara, 5
Sakkayaditthi, 12
Sakridagami, 30, 31
Sakyamuni, 2, 5, 9, 37, 72, 73, 78, 94, 105
Salvation, 9, 92, 93
Samadhi, 36
Sambhoga-Kaya, 88
Sambodhi, 7
Samma-Sambuddha, 80
Sangha, 44
San-Pao, 17
Sanscrit, 1, 7, 95, 100
Sarvanikchepa, 42
Sarwajnan-Wahanse, 80
Sasa, 45
Sattva, 6
Saviour, 92
Schelling, 20
Schopenhauer, 48, 104
Scripture, 9, 18, 19, 20, 26, 43, 45, etc.
Scrota, 28
Scrotapatti, 28, 29
Seh-Shen, 16
Selfhood, 42
Sewet, 51
Shah-Tseh, 32
Shanghai, 74
Shelley, 98
Shen-Ming, 51
Shore, 23, 47
Shravasti, 2, 4, 5
Siao-Fah, 64
Signs, 50
Silver, 25, 43, 64, 108
Singhalese, 78
Siva, 17
Sivaism, 17
Sophocles, 65
Spawn, 9

INDEX

Spirits, 44, 110
Spiritualist, 48
Sramana, 36
S'ruti, 1
Sthula, 83
Subhuti, 5, 8, 13, etc.
Sugata, 26
Sujata, 70
Sumeru, 40, 42, 58
Sutana, 2
Sutra, 1, 8, 27, 45, 47, 68, 77, 91, 92, 108
Sutta-Nipata, 23, 27, 66
Swastika, 50
Syria, 20
Sz-ti, 32

Ta-Chen-Che, 62
Talents, 78
Tang (dynasty), 76
Ta-Pi-Ku, 3
Tathagata, 25, 26, 38, 47, 49, 59, 63, 72, etc.
Teacher, 3
Temples, 39
Tennyson, 23
Thomson (J. Cockburn), 8, 23, 34, 58, 68
Ti-Ching, 11
Tien, 44
Tien-Kong, 30
Ting-Kwang-Fuh, 37
Topes, 64
Treasures, 25, 43, 64, 81, 91, 108

Trimurti, 17
Triratna, 17
Truth, 27, 78, 79
Tsz-Ran-Chioh-Sing, 25
Tuchita, 5
Twan-Tsi-Sin-Yao, 76

Upadanas, 13

Vagrakkhedika (The), 25, 26, 28, 30, 39, 42, 45, 47, etc.
Vais'ali, 5
Vedas, 1
Vedic, 89
Vice, 3
Vihara, 109
Virtue, 3
Vows, 19

Waddhaktinka, 4
Waterfall, 86
Water-strainer, 3
West, 110
Wiharas, 51
Williams (Sir Monier), 49, 63, 66, 84
Wisdom, 3, 7, 8, 47
Wou-Wei, 24
Wu-Wei, Fah, 28

Yen-Ping, 87
Yogi, 20
Yojanas, 109
Yuan-Chioh-Sutra, 100

Printed at
The Edinburgh Press,
9 & 11 Young Street.

Printed in the United States
64252LVS00001BC/37